Putting Knowledge Networks into Action

Methodology, Development, Maintenance

Andrea Back · Georg von Krogh
Andreas Seufert · Ellen Enkel
Editors

Putting Knowledge Networks into Action

Methodology, Development, Maintenance

With Contributions by

Andreas Seufert, Ellen Enkel, Jörg Raimann
Stefanos Vassiliadis, Yvonne Wicki
Andrea Back, Georg von Krogh

Springer

Professor Dr. Andrea Back
IWI-HSG – Institute of Information Management
University of St. Gallen
Müller-Friedberg-Strasse 8
9000 St. Gallen
Switzerland
E-mail: andrea.back@unisg.ch

Professor Dr. Andreas Seufert
Ludwigshafen University of Applied Sciences
Department 1 – Management and Controlling
Ernst-Boehe-Strasse 4
67059 Ludwigshafen
Germany
E-mail: Andreas.Seufert@fh-ludwigshafen.de

Professor Dr. Georg von Krogh
IfB-HSG – Institute of Management
University of St. Gallen
Dufourstrasse 40a
9000 St. Gallen
Switzerland
E-mail: georg.vonkrogh@unisg.ch

Dr. Ellen Enkel
ITEM-HSG – Institute of Technology Management
University of St. Gallen
Dufourstrasse 40a
9000 St. Gallen
Switzerland
E-mail: ellen.enkel@unisg.ch

With 38 Figures and 18 Tables

Library of Congress Control Number: 2005922174

ISBN 3-540-40574-7 Springer Berlin Heidelberg New York

Springer is a part of Springer Science+Business Media
springeronline.com

Printed in Germany

Cover design: Erich Kirchner
Production: Helmut Petri
Printing: Strauss Offsetdruck

SPIN 10946039 Printed on acid-free paper – 42/3153 – 5 4 3 2 1 0

Table of Content

INTRODUCTION **1**

1 MANAGEMENT SUMMARY **3**

2 AT A GLANCE - COMPETING THROUGH KNOWLEDGE NETWORKS **7**

2.1 INTERCONNECT BUSINESS STRATEGY AND KNOWLEDGE NETWORKS 8
2.2 INTERCONNECT KNOWLEDGE WORK PROCESSES AND KNOWLEDGE NETWORK ARCHITECTURE 9
2.3 INTERCONNECT KNOWLEDGE WORK PROCESSES AND FACILITATING CONDITIONS 10

3 ABOUT THIS HANDBOOK **13**

3.1 OBJECTIVE 13
3.2 RESEARCH MODEL 14
3.3 STRUCTURE OF THE HANDBOOK 15

4 BUILDING BLOCKS **17**

4.1 OVERVIEW 17
4.2 BUSINESS STRATEGY AND KNOWLEDGE NETWORKS 21
4.2.1 Interlinkage of Business Strategy and Knowledge Networks 21
4.2.2 Using Knowledge Networks to Transform Business Strategy into Action 25
4.3 KNOWLEDGE NETWORK REFERENCE TYPES 30
4.3.1 Derivation of Knowledge Network Reference Types 31
4.3.2 Facilitating Conditions 38
4.3.3 Knowledge Network Architecture 47
4.3.4 Blueprints of Knowledge Network Reference Types 61
4.3.5 Knowledge Network Reference Type Experiencing Network 62
4.3.6 Knowledge Network Reference Type Materializing Network 66
4.3.7 Knowledge Network Reference Type Systematizing Network 70
4.3.8 Knowledge Network Reference Type Learning Network 74

4.4 A Knowledge Network Scorecard and Health Check 79
4.4.1 Introduction 79
4.4.2 An Integrated Measurement System 80
4.4.3 Health Check of the Knowledge Network 90

5 STORYBOARD – SETTING UP KNOWLEDGE NETWORKS......97

5.1 Introduction 97
5.2 Clarify the Knowledge Vision 99
5.3 Decide on the Network Option 102
5.3.1 Identify Your Knowledge Strategy 103
5.3.2 Select and Understand a Process or Task 104
5.3.3 Perform a Stakeholder Analysis 106
5.3.4 Understand the Different Types of Knowledge Needed 107
5.3.5 Decide on the Network Option 109
5.4 Select the Appropriate Network Reference Type 112
5.4.1 Types of Operational Knowledge Tasks and Types of Knowledge Created 113
5.4.2 The Facilitating Conditions Determine the Knowledge Network Reference Type 115
5.4.3 Identified Deliverables Determine the Appropriate Knowledge Network 118
5.5 Set Up the Selected Knowledge Network 121
5.5.1 Start-up 122
5.5.2 Mapping Processes and Roles 127
5.5.3 Facilitate Relationships to the Outside World 150
5.5.4 Establish Internal Measurement 156
5.6 Measure and Adapt the Knowledge Network 166
5.6.1 Internal Knowledge Network Measurement System 167

6 SUMMARY AND ACTION PLAN 177

7 LIST OF FIGURES 181

8 LIST OF TABLES 183

9 INDEX 185

10 REFERENCES 187

Introduction

The concepts and theories of knowledge management and networks are about to become well documented. Yet there are few, if any, guidelines on how to implement knowledge management within an organization, especially focusing on how to manage knowledge in a network environment. On the one hand, this is paraphrasing Tom Stewart's assertion in his book, Intellectual Capital, that nobody knows how to write a cookbook with knowledge management recipes, and on the other hand, it reinforces that managing knowledge in networks is a rather new and unexplored field.

However, in the case of some organizations, paths have emerged that yielded benefits. This handbook visualizes those paths which allow to connect theories, concepts, and concrete actions. Managing knowledge in network environments is a fast-moving field attempting to integrate various disciplines, such as human resources, organizational development, change management, strategy, information technology, sociology, and network theory. The objective of this book is to integrate these different roots into a holistic view on managing knowledge in networks. Therefore we develop a methodology, which will support you to move concrete steps forward towards building and maintaining knowledge networks in your organization.

1 Management Summary

> *"In an economy where the only certainty is uncertainty, the one sure source of lasting competitive advantage is knowledge." (Nonaka, 1991).*

Knowledge is increasingly recognized by modern organizations as their most important source of lasting competitive advantage. However, the key to obtaining long-term competitive advantages is not to be found in the administration of existing knowledge, but in the ability to constantly generate new knowledge, and to move on to new products and services. Rather than viewing firms as devices for processing information, making decisions, and solving problems, it should be realized that they are increasingly based on knowledge seeking and knowledge creation.

Therefore, we believe that at least two aspects are crucial. First, knowledge management should comprise a holistic view of knowledge, that is to say, the integration of explicit and implicit knowledge. Second, knowledge management should take a holistic view on where and how knowledge is being created and transferred. Knowledge is often thought of as an objective commodity that is transferable, independent of person and context. On the basis of this mental model, people often try to solve problems by just improving the information processing by intensively using modern technologies, such as intranet-based yellow pages, knowledge maps, or information warehouses. The potential of innovative technologies for the mastery and distribution of explicit knowledge, i.e., knowledge that is pinned down verbally in writing or electronically and can therefore be easily communicated and distributed; is undisputed. However, what is required is an integrated approach that includes both, explicit and implicit (tacit) knowledge. Since implicit knowledge is deeply rooted in personal experiences, subjective insights, and values and feelings, communicating and sharing it is challenging. Tacit knowledge can be conceptualized in terms of technical and cognitive dimensions. Whereas the technical dimension contains informal, personal skills and capabilities, often designated as "know-how", the cognitive dimension includes mental models influenced by people's beliefs, values, and convictions.

> *"The focus shifts from products and firms as units of analysis to people, organizations, and the social processes that bind together in ongoing relationships." (Webster, 1992, p. 10).*

Organizations are more and more changing from well structured and manageable systems into interwoven network systems with blurred boundaries. Genuine sharing of authorities takes place. Firms are neither fully independent nor is one wholly dependent upon another. They do not lose their legal identities; they retain their own culture and management structure and can pursue their own strategies. But they do have to reduce their autonomy, share decision-making, interconnect their organization structure, jointly manage some activities or operations, and open their company culture to external influences. Assuming this evolution to be the trend for future organizations, we must - from a knowledge management perspective – perceive managing knowledge creation and transfer as taking place in the context of a network, rather than view it from a traditional organizational perspective. Since we believe this network perspective to be key for the future of knowledge management, we conceptualize an integrated view of what we call knowledge networking. We develop a framework and point out the implications for management.

> *"Most important, in an age of rapidly proliferating knowledge, the central domain is a social network that absorbs, creates, transforms, buys, sells, and communicates knowledge. Its stronghold is the knowledge embedded in a dense web of social, economic, contractual, and administrative relationships." (Badaracco, 1991, pp. 13-14).*

For this reason a network should be built up in which the knowledge and experience of employees are made available in order to make effective use of knowledge. It is of primary importance that not just the mere accumulation of data but creating and sharing processes are encouraged.

Focusing only on explicit knowledge, as well as having a limited view of work, learning, and innovation, involves the danger of erecting various barriers: functional and hierarchical; barriers to customers, suppliers and co-operation partners; or mental barriers which impede the creation, transfer, and flow of knowledge. These barriers do not only hinder the short-term flow but also the long term flow of knowledge, which could prove detrimental to a company's innovation and learning ability. Based on an integrated knowledge management approach, knowledge networking may deliver a conceptual framework for rethinking the knowledge management model. In this case, knowledge barriers should be overcome by "networking" and knowledge islands should be cross-linked in order to stimulate the evolution, dissemination, and application of knowledge.

The integration of networking into knowledge management yields great benefits. The openness and richness of networks are believed to foster a fertile environment for the creation of entirely new knowledge, while also accelerating the innovation rate. Additionally, reliance on networks has potential transforming effects on all participants. Those positioned in a network adopt more innovations and are likely to do so sooner. The presence of a dense network of collaborative ties may even alter participants' views on competition. Within a densely connected field, people have to adapt to a novel perspective in which it is no longer necessary to have exclusive ownership of an asset in order to profit from it.

2 At a Glance - Competing through Knowledge Networks

Knowledge networks may be understood as social networks between knowledge players, which allow the creation and transfer of knowledge among individuals, groups, organizations, and between hierarchical levels.

Definition

Knowledge Network

A knowledge network represents a number of people, resources, and the relationships among them, which are assembled to accumulate and use knowledge, primarily through knowledge creation and transfer processes, for the ultimate purpose of creating value. Thus, a network may evolve whose participants share a common language and a common set of values and objectives. This social network is supported and transformed by information and communication technology (ICT). Since this network of knowledge resources is being continuously augmented by knowledge gained from learning situations, a knowledge network should be regarded as a dynamic structure rather than as a static institution.

From the management perspective, we consider the following interface functions to yield great benefits for managing knowledge in networks:

- Interconnect business strategy and knowledge networks by interlinking different levels and areas of knowledge.
- Interconnect knowledge work processes and knowledge network architecture.
- Interconnect knowledge work processes and facilitating conditions.

2.1 Interconnect Business Strategy and Knowledge Networks

Knowledge results from networking, using previous knowledge with new knowledge. Therefore, it is essential to enable networking between individual knowledge types (explicit and implicit) and between the different levels (e.g. individual, group, organization) and areas of knowledge (e.g. customer knowledge, R&D knowledge). This is more important when organizations rapidly increase in size and networks can be regarded as key to finding critical organizational knowledge. Companies often attach importance to the involvement of people whose mandate is to keep tabs on who knows what and to help others find their way to the appropriate internal resource.

Profile **McKinsey & Company**

> *Our culture has always placed a heavy premium on what people know. The flip side is that people are sensitive to acknowledge what they know. The message that establishing the RRN sent was, "It's OK if you can't do it alone".*

During the 1980s, McKinsey & Company, one of the world's most prestigious consulting firms, experienced exponential growth. Not surprisingly, the firm's size increased, and the diffusion of expertise rapidly ensued. After decades of being a relatively intimate network of professionals, McKinsey was suddenly a truly global firm, where partners did not to necessarily get to know each other, and picking up the telephone was no longer the quickest way towards an answer to a pressing client problem.

In 1989, McKinsey launched the Rapid Response Network (RRN), a dispersed team of professionals knowledgeable about the field of organizational consulting. The RRN had software support in the form of a request tracking database and a resource database which included the best thinking – both inside and outside the firm – in addition to information about who in the firm were leading thinkers in this particular area. "The RRN constituted a real shift for McKinsey," says Phil Terry, Manager of New Media and Knowledge Systems.

The RRN team exemplified this philosophy. Although a virtual network, it was a close-knit unit of people who supported one another. Knowledge exchange within the group was considered a key factor in developing an understanding of organizational design and the strategy work going on across McKinsey. Within the organization practice – a function specialty that crosses all industries – there are nine or ten sub-areas (e.g., human resources, culture, change management, leadership), and each of these sub-areas has a knowledge manager. Knowledge managers sit at the center of McKinsey's various practice communities, not only overseeing web site content, but also interacting with a network of consultants and practice leaders to create the links that define the community. The knowledge manager also serves as an "informed layer" that sits between the information specialist, whose primary function is to find information, and the expert consultants, who directly serve clients on organizational issues, and are held in reserve to help with highly specialized or complex questions (Bukowitz and Williams, 1999).

2.2 Interconnect Knowledge Work Processes and Knowledge Network Architecture

Knowledge creation and transfer can occur at various real (e.g. in the office, with the customer), virtual (e.g. distributed team rooms), or mental (e.g. common values, ideas, ideals) places. They can establish themselves as formal or informal networks. Therefore, finding expertise in large organizations can be an arduous and confusing experience, full of blind alleys and wrong turns. Since knowledge creation and transfer occurs more and more in different time-zones and different physical places, the success of a knowledge network lies in a firm's ability to effectively use modern information and communication technologies.

Profile **Chevron**

We're moving closer to an organizational understanding of expertise at Chevron. And the closer we get, the more people, teams, and communities of practice are coming forward of their own accord.

In 1994, global oil giant Chevron formalized its efforts to share best practices across its business units by introducing new tools to the organization on a worldwide basis. Among these tools was a best practice database, which used a process approach to organizing best practice content. At the same time, many different units (including the corporate group) within all business entities had launched their own initiatives for sharing best practice ideas. Their approaches ranged from networks and best

practice teams to databases, workshops, and conferences. The challenge was to bring all these activities together.
Instead of mandating all individual initiatives to be centralized, the company hit on another approach – a Best Practice Resource Map that could point people, who were interested in finding out more about best practices, at certain existing resources and groups that already had initiatives in place. Its color-coded main categories comprise the seven criteria from the Baldrige Award, which are also used in Chevron's quality review process. Within each process category is a list of resources with brief descriptions of the resource, a reference to the pertinent organization within Chevron, and the name of a person to contact for further information. This is to promote cross-fertilization of ideas by putting teams working on similar issues in touch with each other. "The best practice resource map is a great pointer to team-based initiatives," says quality consultant Patricia Wagner. "Going forward, our vision is to better identify both, the team and the individual expertise." Chevron's best practices database allows teams and individuals to contribute their best practices immediately, by filling out a standardized form. Submissions are helping to make an organization's expertise more visible and more accessible. Ultimately, the database will point at people with specific knowledge (Bukowitz and Williams, 1999).

2.3 Interconnect Knowledge Work Processes and Facilitating Conditions

In order to implement effective knowledge processes, they have to be adapted and cross-linked to the surroundings in which they are embedded. On the one hand, these processes must be coordinated with the environment and the corporate culture in which they occur. On the other hand, the companies should actively develop and maintain supportive surroundings; i.e., facilitating conditions, in order to enable and support efficient and effective knowledge flows.

Profile IBM Global Services

> *"At IBM Global Services, these networks are logical gatekeepers for specialized knowledge." Individuals are encouraged to maintain ownership. Ownership carries out both the benefit of being an acknowledged expert and the responsibility of fielding questions and keeping the knowledge up to date.*

IBM Global Services is the division of computer giant IBM that includes a range of service-based businesses, including consulting, systems integration, outsourcing, product support services, e-business and learning services. In the mid-1990s, the consulting business instituted a knowledge management which was so successful that it has expanded to about 40 people worldwide, who are now responsible for increasing the level of knowledge contribution and its use throughout the entire division.

A key organizing framework for this knowledge usage is the division's knowledge networks. They focus on an industry, such as automotive; a technology, such as SAP; a business area, such as e-business; or even a process, such as project management.

Each network has a leader and a core team – a group of eight to ten people who spend about 10% of their time managing the networks' intellectual capital and knowledge. When people contribute intellectual capital it is presented to the core team that deals with the question "How can we package this knowledge so that it is most useful to the network?"

Every piece of intellectual capital that is electronically made available to the network has a contact name. Generally, this is the name of the original contributor. Each contribution contributes to two goals. First, it interlinks interested parties with a more in-depth information source. Second, it gives credit to the originator. In order to be the acknowledged owner, the contributor must be willing to take phone calls or answer e-mails regarding his or her contribution. If contributors do not want to take on this responsibility, then a member of the core team becomes the owner. Knowledge networks are explicitly acknowledged groups at IBM, sponsored by a business unit. Once a group is sponsored, the leader contacts the knowledge management team, which then assigns a relationship manager to thc group.

The relationship manager's responsibility is to work with the network's core team to develop a strategy and plan for managing the network's intellectual capital. The first step in this process is to define the networks' business priorities and strategic initiatives. Then, the team identifies members of the network. The network needs to be global in scope, attracting the "best of the best" who can contribute expertise related to a practice area. Next, the team works with its relationship manager, both virtually and face to face, to define the network's domain of knowledge – specifically what the network requires to operate and what knowledge resources it will need. The group then engages in a hunting and harvesting exercise, determining what knowledge already exists and developing an action plan to gather what knowledge resources it will need. The relationship manager also takes the core team through a crash course on knowledge management. The objective here is to show the group how knowledge management can help achieve its business goals. Once the core team has set operating guidelines and has assigned roles and responsibilities, it is ready to launch this to network members. The role of the core team members has gone through several iterations at IBM. Initially, they were paid out of a central budget because the community development process was introduced mid-year, and without the ability to bill for their time, core members would have been penalized. However, in 1997 bonus incentives were put in place worldwide to recognize and reward core team participation. Performance criteria were also developed for the communities themselves (Bukowitz and Williams, 1999).

3 About this Handbook

3.1 Objective

The knowledge network handbook is a guide for people who are:

- already familiar with the concept of knowledge management,
- convinced that networks are of ever increasing importance in the future,
- committed to action and want to know what to do next.

You will not find a detailed argumentation on the importance of knowledge management, or the justification for embarking on knowledge management activities in this book. We assume that you already accept the necessity to think more closely about and better manage the flow of knowledge throughout your organization. In the case you would like to read or refer to literature that extensively traces the emergence of the knowledge management movement and its rationale, we have provided you with a selected bibliography at the end of the handbook, which lists some excellent sources. What you will find in this book is a robust approach based on the strategies and operations of pioneering organizations, which are using knowledge networks to improve their business performance.

We also assume that you are beyond the point of questioning whether or not you should do something about the management of knowledge in networks. People responsible for constructing an organizational response to the knowledge network challenge come from a wide range of functional and operational groups. Yet it seems to us that these numerous different functional and operating paths all lead to one organizational intersection: the creation and transfer of knowledge within network environments in order to increase the company's value.

To sum up, the purpose of the knowledge network handbook is to offer you a framework for thinking about the network approach for managing knowledge and to guide your concrete implementation steps.

3.2 Research Model

The competence center knowledge networks is a research project within the research center KnowledgeSource which was co-founded by Prof. Dr. Georg von Krogh (Institute of Management), Prof. Dr. Andrea Back (Institute for Information Management), and Dr. Andreas Seufert (Institute for Information Management) at the University of St. Gallen (HSG). Within the framework of an international research cooperation with business and research partners, the objective of KnowledgeSource is to develop an integrated approach to strategic and information management in order to achieve lasting competitive advantages through knowledge management. In cooperation with its industry partners DaimlerChrysler, Hewlett Packard, Lotus Professional Services, and Unilever the competence center focuses its research activities towards an integrated view of knowledge management and networking. The main objectives of the CC KNN are to establish a shared understanding, a reference model, and a methodology, for building high performing knowledge networks. These results aim at supporting our partner corporations in the process of establishing, recognizing, and facilitating knowledge networks within their organizations. To achieve this goal, the reference model and methodology are mainly based on academic research, bilateral projects with our partner corporations, as well as case studies from reputable organizations. Figure 1 provides an overview of the underlying research design.

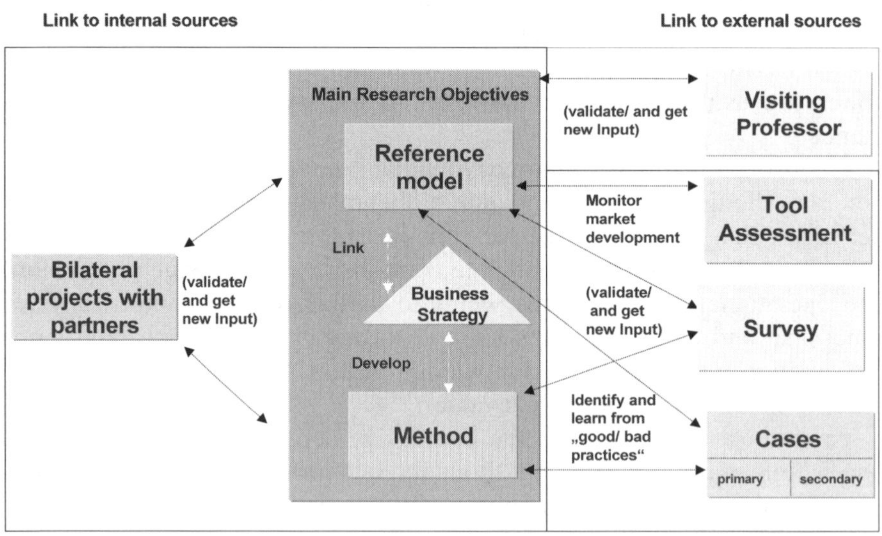

Fig. 1. Research design

Starting with the joint development of the first version of a reference model for knowledge networks, this model was further validated and developed thanks to bilateral projects in practice, as well as to discussions and workshops with visiting professors at the competence center (Winter 1998 Prof. Nonaka, Hitotsubashi/ Berkley; Summer 1999 Prof. Cusumano/ MIT and Winter 1999/2000 Prof. Singh/ Wharton).

3.3 Structure of the Handbook

The handbook consists of two main parts:

- Part I: Building Blocks
- Part II: Storyboard – Setting Up Knowledge Networks

In part I, Building Blocks, we provide an overview of the key elements of the methodology. We start with describing and interlinking business strategy and knowledge networks. After that we develop knowledge network reference types which might serve as blueprints for the implementation. Based on the characteristics of knowledge networks we then elaborate on the specifics for each type. Finally, we outline an approach to measure the knowledge network activities.

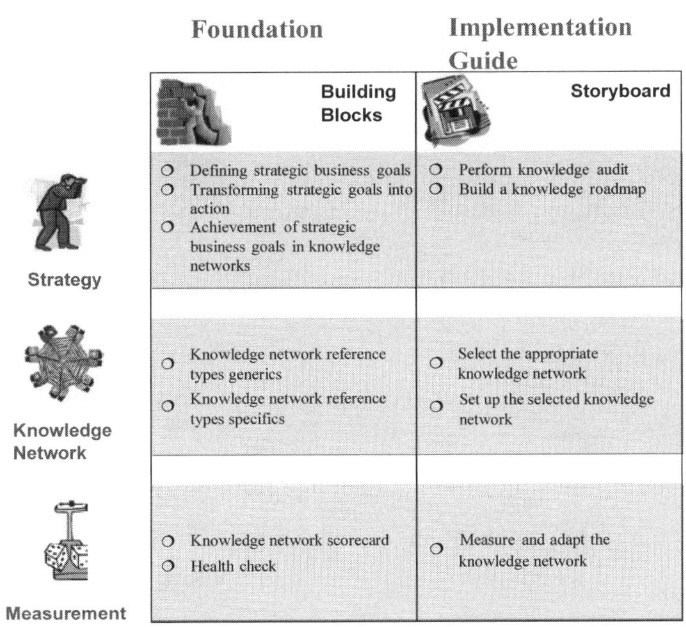

Fig. 2. Structure of the handbook

Part II, Storyboard, covers the procedural model of the methodology. In this section we describe the process steps of set up and maintenance of a knowledge network. Additionally we give concrete suggestions on what should be considered at which point in time.

Since we are aware of the limitations associated with a sequential book structure, we try to help you to select the chapters that you are especially interested in by using a "reading configurator". We consider this as a guide through this manual in order to support the reader while navigating through and interlinking defined result sets.

4 Building Blocks

4.1 Overview

The following chapter introduces the building blocks of the methodology. It encompasses a description of the key elements that are used in the storyboard and their interrelations. Based on these elements the storyboard guides through the steps to examine the company's business environment and its current status in order to recommend company specific steps for setting up a knowledge network.

The building blocks of the methodology consist of the following three areas:

- Business strategy and knowledge networks.
- Knowledge network reference types.
- Knowledge network scorecard and health check.

Knowledge is a key resource to achieve competitive advantages. Therefore our model focuses on the business processes which are derived from the business strategy. From this perspective, strategy serves as a starting point for defining the requirements that need to be fulfilled by a knowledge network. In practice a concrete task or process might serve as a starting point as well. Based on our research we can subsume all possible business goals under the following three categories: risk optimization, efficiency, and innovation.

Knowledge networks are a type of organizational environment in which knowledge management activities take place. They consist of three layers; the knowledge work processes, the knowledge network architecture to support these processes, and the facilitating conditions; that is to say, the environment in which the knowledge processes – embedded in business processes – take place. Research has shown that there are different types of knowledge networks that can be identified and described using different characteristics. These knowledge network reference types will serve as blueprints for building a knowledge network.

Since knowledge networks are an organizational form in which knowledge processes take place in order to achieve the predetermined business goals, coordination of business strategy, and the knowledge network types, is essential. You should bear in mind that this interrelation is reciprocal, meaning that a certain organizational form will also have an influence on the strategy of the company. From a market-based perspective, business strategy defines the business goals that have to be addressed by the knowledge network. On the other hand, a certain set of resources is required to achieve these business goals. Since in most organizations the market-based view is predominant for the organizational design, networks are a useful approach to combine, integrate, and link knowledge resources with business tasks. The knowledge network reference types hereby serve as an outline in order to get an impression of the resources required.

As shown in figure 3 this has two effects. On the one hand networks help to bridge organizational functions that are usually not interlinked by building a space for knowledge creation and transfer. On the other hand these knowledge networks directly support knowledge intensive business processes by providing access to relevant knowledge in terms of fulfilling a specific knowledge operational task.

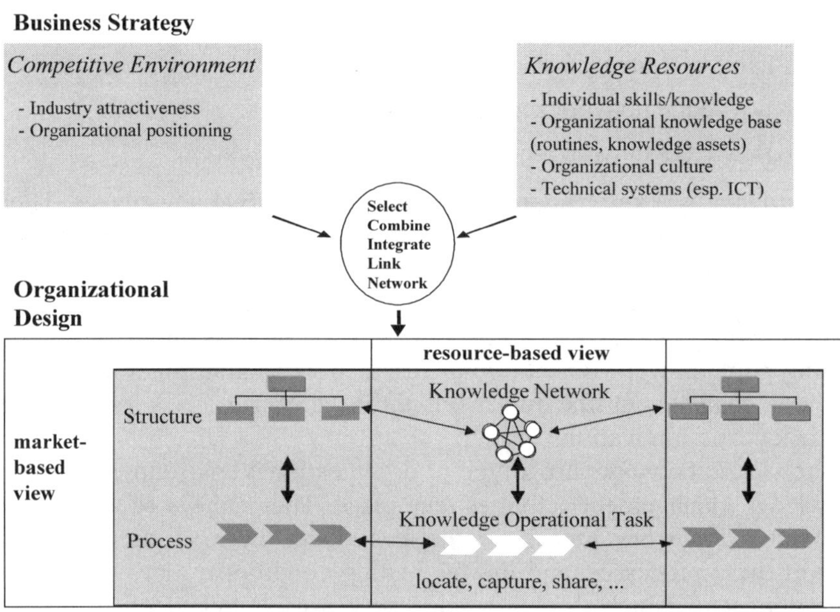

Fig. 3. Business strategy and knowledge networks

Definition

Knowledge Operational Task

The main knowledge transformation process pursued by a knowledge network is called a knowledge operational task.

We identify specific types of knowledge networks according to their knowledge operational tasks:

1. Dealing with the transformation of implicit knowledge (identification and so forth) into other implicit knowledge (experiencing network).
2. Dealing with the transformation of implicit knowledge into explicit knowledge (materializing network).
3. Dealing with the transformation of explicit knowledge into other explicit knowledge (which is of higher value) (resystematizing network).
4. Dealing with the transformation of explicit knowledge into implicit knowledge (learning network).

These knowledge network reference types are described according to the specific characteristics that are required to accomplish the derived business task or to support the business processes. For this purpose we describe the specific tools (ICT and organizational tools) which serve to optimize the work of the network reference type.

Every network reference type is influenced by its facilitating conditions, especially by the organizational structure and the culture of the company. According to Giddens' structuration theory (Giddens, 1984), social actors are reproducing the conditions that determine their actions within and through their action. Furthermore, these structures are the medium for, as well as the result of, social actions. Thus, the knowledge network will influence the culture of the company, while at the same time the company will be influenced by it. As a result, some characteristics of the networks depend on the specific culture and organizational structure of the company. For example, the frequency of communication, the network topology, the size of the network, the environment in which interactions within networks primarily take place (virtual or face-to-face), in addition to the selection of the optimal incentives and performance measures, are all exogenous variables in this sense.

Finally, the knowledge network scorecard measures the impact of the implemented knowledge network. The knowledge network's performance is measured on a company, a network, and later on an individual level, and is determined by the degree of goal achievement. In order to capture the relevant aspects concerning individual performance appraisal, the knowledge network health check will also be introduced. Thereby, we suggest a system that measures the output of the knowledge network in relation to the initial business goals, and integrates quantitative as well as qualitative factors. This will be elaborated on in the subsequent chapters. The following figure gives an overview of the building blocks and their interconnections.

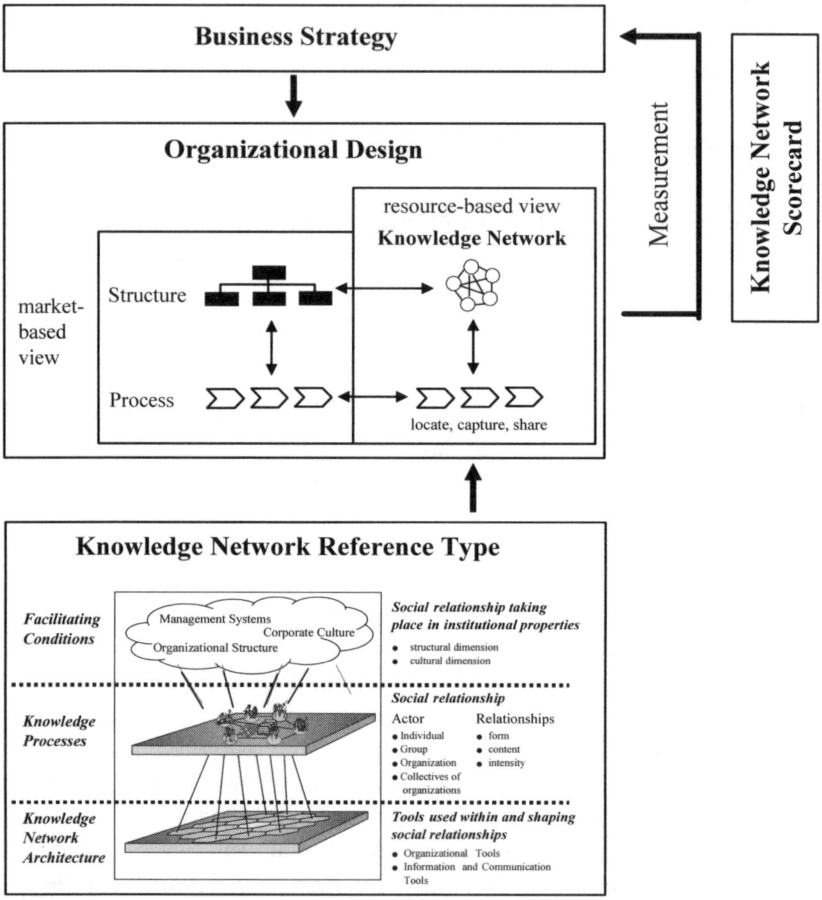

Fig. 4. Building blocks of the methodology

4.2 Business Strategy and Knowledge Networks

Strategy

4.2.1 Interlinkage of Business Strategy and Knowledge Networks

Modern management doctrine has shown in theory as well as in practice that it is especially middle- and long-term goals, such as efficiency improvement, increased innovation, and risk optimization (von Krogh et al., 1999) which lead to sustainable competitive advantage (Bleicher, 1991; Porter, 1985; Prahalad and Hamel, 1990).

There are also many indications in literature that the discipline of knowledge management is most successful, when it deals with middle- and long-term goals (Nonaka and Takeuchi, 1995; Senge, 1994; von Krogh and Roos, 1996; von Krogh and Venzin, 1995). The aim of the strategic goals is to give a framework when developing and choosing a strategy, especially a knowledge strategy. Through the alignment of the knowledge advancement activities with all the business units' strategic goals, it should be made sure that the local efforts help to carry out the strategy of the company. According to the business strategy, a business goal and some specific business processes are selected. In the following three strategic goals will be discussed: efficiency improvement, increased innovation, and risk optimization.

Profile **Texas Instruments**

In the beginning of the 90s Texas Instruments was confronted with consistent delays in its product delivery. In order to solve this problem, a project team was established to search for best practices inside the company. Through the transfer of these best practices between the various units of the company, it was possible not only to minimize delays, but also to reduce the delivery costs (O'Dell and Grayson, 1998).

The main focus of efficiency improvement is to reduce the costs in the existing business processes quicker than the competitors. On company level, it is about achieving higher efficiency by increasing the value of the output in relation to the costs of the input. For many companies, one of the greatest challenges is the improvement of their business processes and the transfer to other parts of the company (von Krogh et al., 1999).

Increased efficiency in operation can also mean improving the speed of processes, getting the "right" types and amount of processes, improving decision making, and increasing responsiveness to customers. In this respect it is also essential to learn from partners, competitors, and other departments, how to manage the business processes more efficiently.

The goal of risk optimization mainly concerns the risks associated with investments and operating the business. Many companies face at least two main risks: political and competitive (von Krogh et al., 1999). The political risk is a result of uncertainty regarding political decisions. Especially for international companies this can bear a big challenge, since national governments can often make unexpected decisions which cannot be influenced by the company. Competitive risks depend on the uncertainty surrounding the actions and reactions of existing competitors, as well as that of emerging competitors. Since many companies operate in more than one market, and since the boundaries of these markets erode, anticipating such changes becomes increasingly difficult.

Profile **Aerospace**

In order to reduce its competitive risks, the German company Aerospace created a simulation program that incorporated possible future environmental conditions in its core businesses. The managers in the company were thus able to learn to recognize and understand the complexity and the interplay of environmental conditions that can have an effect on their business (Schüppel, 1996). Hence, new knowledge about alternative future scenarios and the functions in the competitive environments was created, reducing the competitive risk of the company.

Other risks a company might face are:

1. *Knowledge risk*, which is the risk of not having the correct knowledge at the right place at the right time.
2. *Financial risk*, which is the risk of the business not managing its finances appropriately.
3. *Human risk*, which is the risk that the business does not employ the right people for the tasks, and that employees with valuable knowledge leave.
4. *Derived demand risk*, which is the risk that the business either misunderstands or ignores potentially profitable new technologies, or does not engage in sufficient innovation to offset future competition.

5. *Communication risk*, which is the risk that the business does not sufficiently communicate its accomplishments to the market and to the other stakeholders.
6. *Customer risk*, which is the risk that customers are not correctly managed, and that customer satisfaction decreases, resulting in lower repeat and referred business.
7. *Structural risk*, which is the risk that the business cannot support current management initiatives due to a deficient structure.
8. *Resource risk*, which is the risk of not having the needed resources to implement the company's strategy. Managing the company's risk exposure can also mean capturing the knowledge of experts before retirement, avoiding over-taxing local resources by transferring key personnel on demand, and learning from your projects in order to avoid repeated mistakes.

Increased innovation is about improving one's competitive position through product, service, and process innovations (von Krogh et al., 1999). Innovations are mostly based on procedural knowledge and cultural conditions which are not easily imitable by competitors. Procedural knowledge is knowledge that has something to do with the generic innovation processes. Such a process consists of different phases, such as concept development, evaluation and selection of alternatives, and development of prototypes (Nonaka and Takeuchi, 1995). Cultural conditions encompass shared values and modes of behavior within the company (von Krogh et al., 1998). For larger companies with many business units, the challenge is to leverage their procedural knowledge to develop different innovations throughout the company and thus achieve a sustainable competitive advantage. Ultimately, innovation is about creating new sources of revenues through new products and services. In the long run, companies ought to develop a culture that encourages innovation. An innovation culture facilitates the development of many different products within a short period of time (Widmer, 1999).

Profile **Eisai**

Eisai, a large pharmaceutical company in Japan, realized that they produced medicine, but did not know anything about healthcare. They did not have any knowledge on how their products were used. To overcome this knowledge gap, they introduced a three day "Preceptorship Program" at an elderly nursing hospital, where managers had to help with bathing, feeding, and other personal care. 590 managers participated in this program. The aim was to gain implicit knowledge by realizing the needs of elderly people in order to gain a better understanding of the aspects involved in administering a drug. Among other things, the participants found out that elderly people drink very little water and have problems with swallowing big pills (some of the Eisai pills are considered "horse pills"). Thus, often the elderly people did not take the pills, but rather put them into the flower pot, once the nurse was gone. Based on this experience, Eisai started to develop innovative products that could be integrated into the food.

For innovation it is essential to capture new business process and innovation ideas throughout the company, to adapt a new product or marketing instrument to another part of the company, and to create in-depth knowledge to develop radical innovation and process improvements. Having discussed the strategic business goals, we will in the following turn our focus to the central knowledge processes and the evolution of knowledge management.

Key Issue: Managing the Knowledge Flow

From a strategic perspective it is crucial to realize that knowledge is never idle. It flows continuously from activity to activity, from person to person, from task to task, and from system to system. From this observation the need arises for an analysis of the various business processes and the underlying knowledge processes. Although these processes are often strongly linked to each other and also influence each other, it was proven helpful to create generic categories of these knowledge processes.

First, it is possible to divide knowledge management into logical phases of evolution through these categories. Second, these categories help to identify knowledge barriers and develop knowledge enhancing measures.

Knowledge processes can be classified into three categories: (1) localizing and capturing, (2) sharing and transferring, (3) creating and applying.

Localizing and capturing knowledge means finding and charting already existing knowledge in the company. This is a big challenge, especially for companies that have a widely dispersed knowledge base. In these companies business units often encounter problems that have already been solved in another part of the company. Since they are not aware of these solutions, they are forced to reinvent the wheel over and over again. Localizing and capturing existing knowledge helps to find answers to actual problems. Consequently, professional knowledge management must create clarity regarding the existing knowledge base of the company. Because of the enormous advances of ICT technologies, there are many possibilities to support knowledge identification. Many companies have developed "knowledge maps" and "yellow pages," which dramatically reduce search costs. This is especially helpful in large, diversified companies, where experts can be localized despite geographical dispersion.

Knowledge sharing and transferring refers to the leveraging of existing knowledge in groups, teams, divisions, and business units, in order to generate value for the company. Explicit knowledge can often be easily transferred through electronic media or other forms of documents such as manuals and handbooks. Sharing implicit knowledge, in contrary, is more difficult, since direct interaction of the people within the organization is crucial (Brown and Duguid, 1991; Leonard and Sensiper, 1998; Leonard-Barton, 1995; von Krogh and Köhne, 1998). Knowledge can be embodied in stories, actions, metaphors, analogies, behaviors, or visions. The process of knowledge creation deals with the development of new explicit or implicit knowledge by groups or individuals, which has not already been existing in the company. New knowledge can be created either through the expansion of already existing implicit or explicit knowledge, or through a new method of combining these forms of knowledge. Nonaka (1991; 1999; Nonaka and Konno, 1998; Nonaka et al., 1998; Nonaka and Takeuchi, 1995) divides the process of knowledge creation into four different subprocesses: combination, externalization, socialization, and internalization.

Finally, the knowledge process applying comprises the application and usage of the knowledge in actual business situations such as decision making or problem solving.

Most companies concentrate on already existing knowledge within the company. Their main activities, in this respect, are localizing and capturing the knowledge of the company. As next step, they start to support processes that help to transfer existing knowledge across organizational divisions and create completely new knowledge. In this context, it is important to mention that the ability to generate new knowledge will play a central role in achieving competitive advantage, since it is precisely this new knowledge that creates a sustainable competitive advantage. Based on these insights three typical stages of knowledge management development can be distinguished that are determined with regard to the investment intensity concerning the relevant activities in each stage.

4.2.2 Using Knowledge Networks to Transform Business Strategy into Action

In the following section, the interconnection between the business process layer, as well as knowledge networks and their tasks, will be described.

The business-oriented perspective assigns a very central role to the business processes of the company describing, among others, the operational layers of procurement, production, and sales/marketing in a company. According to Hammer and Champy (1993), a business process can be defined as a collection of activities that take one or more kinds of input and create an output that is of value for both, the company and the customer. This perspective is also the basis of the value chain concept, which, according to Porter, primarily serves as an analytical instrument for structuring a company into strategically relevant activities (Porter, 1985). A business process can be interlinked to a business function, but just as important, business processes can cut across functional areas and their boundaries (Tanuan, 1997). In total, the company's internal process and service layer can be understood as a framework of business processes and their relationships.

The objective of the knowledge operational task of a knowledge network is to support the business process layer and to create a positive impact to business goals and business strategy.

In principle, all knowledge network reference types can support most business processes. Our study (Enkel and Wicki, 2002) showed that 34% of knowledge management activities strongly support the process of strategic management and 44% strongly support the R&D activities on a corporate level. On the knowledge network level, 40% support the process of strategic management and 58% of knowledge networks support service processes, while only 8% support procurement and 14% support financial management. R&D (36%), technology development (44%) and HRM (20%), are also supported by knowledge networks. The distribution of the business processes supported reflects the actual distribution of industries within our sample. The percentage of service firms could thus explain the high rate of strategic management support, since these companies are more likely to be organized in rather flat, network-like structures. Furthermore, no distinction was found in the survey regarding the different knowledge network reference types. The distribution of the supported business processes was the same within all the knowledge network reference types.

Since knowledge networks can be used to support business processes in many ways, the members of the knowledge network could be directly involved in carrying out the business process. They may execute the entire business process or parts of the process, depending on their specific role (i.e. process owner) in the process. Being directly involved in the business process, the existing knowledge can immediately be made available throughout the network.

Further, knowledge networks can also be indirectly involved in a business process, i.e., as a "supplier" to other business process owners. In this case it is necessary to ensure and facilitate the transfer of the knowledge which is stored (and/or created) in the network.

Knowledge networks can also serve to support the links between several business processes. An example is a knowledge network that ensures the knowledge transfer between two business processes. Members of the knowledge network might directly or indirectly be involved in these business processes. One approach is to link several business processes and/or sub-processes through a knowledge network. Moreover, dependent on the type of business a continuum exists that ranges from standardized processes via semi-structured to so called ad hoc processes. Due to their nature, knowledge networks are in particular suitable for the support and execution of weakly structured processes. However, they might also contribute to specific tasks of highly structured processes.

Profile **ABB**

One example of connecting islands of knowledge is ABB. The company obtained a contract to deliver 32 locomotives of their 2000 type to India within two years. The company, which is organized as a global matrix, used knowledge and technology transfer units which ensured the best possible usage of the knowledge that was developed in more than one country. These units very quickly identified relevant knowledge in Australia, Switzerland, Sweden, and India, and selected a team that could fulfill the contract. This created some sort of knowledge network because the units cut across many organizational boundaries and connected the islands of knowledge in the company. If these units had not been in place, ABB would not have been able to deliver on time.

The potentials of knowledge networks are not limited to business processes. Further networking possibilities are the cross-linking of business units, hierarchical levels, departments, and so forth. In general, knowledge networks can be used to connect "islands of knowledge" across the company, creating in the process an altered form of organization by moving towards a more network-oriented organization.

Knowledge networks serve as storage space for the knowledge. Within a knowledge network, knowledge work processes occur (i.e., locating, capturing, sharing, etc). The knowledge thereby resides in explicit or implicit form in the knowledge network, and can be made available to any business process. The knowledge within the network should not be considered static. It rather "flows" within the network and therefore has a dynamic character. Thus, the transitions from implicit knowledge to explicit knowledge and vice versa are important.

A knowledge network can support more than one business goal. In the previous section we identified three main strategic business goals: efficiency improvement, increased innovation, and risk optimization.

Based on our empirical research (Enkel and Wicki, 2002), we decided to break down these goals by dividing them into sub-categories: increasing productivity and efficiency, cost reduction, reduction of financial risks, reusability of knowledge, increasing the motivation of employees, reduction of human risks, increasing ability to innovate, increasing growth, supporting creativity, and increasing the quality of services and/or products.

On both the corporate and on the network level, the goal of reusing existing knowledge (16% on corporate level and 21% on the network level) and increasing the quality of services or products, are considered the most important (16% on corporate level and 19% on the network level).

Aligning these sub-categories along the three major business goals, our empirical research also showed that all business goals pursued by the corporation and the knowledge network are similar to a certain extent. On both levels, the business goal of increased innovation that determines knowledge activities is present in 35% of the cases. While efficiency improvement is pursued by 39% of the knowledge networks and by 36% of the companies, risk optimization is the main business goal of only 29% of the companies and 26% of the networks. This indicates a similar distribution of the business goals on both, the corporate and network level. In addition, the findings concerning the knowledge network reference types, as well as the classification along the small and large dimensions of networks, supported our hypothesis. From these findings we can draw two conclusions: First, every knowledge network can, at least to a certain extent, support all kinds of business goals and second, the business goals pursued on a corporate level are also pursued to a similar extent on the network level (Enkel and Wicki, 2002).

Key Issue: When to Choose the Network Option?

When contemplating the network choice, there are several questions to consider. In the following, we will outline some general advantages and disadvantages of networks, which should be taken into account when thinking about networks as a strategic choice.

Key Advantages of Networks. Firstly, networks have no boundaries. They cut across the organization and across levels, thereby pushing decision making further down the line. This creates flexibility for faster responses. Within a networked organization individuals know who knows what, and therefore can directly contact experts which results in faster problem-solving. Moreover, networks make it is easier to connect with other colleagues in a large organization to learn about the latest developments.

Since networks are organic in nature, they are flexible and adaptive when environmental conditions require change. This could ultimately lead to new business opportunities. Also, networks are particularly effective in handling and transforming implicit (or tacit) knowledge. This not only constitutes a competitive advantage for the company, since implicit knowledge is difficult to imitate, but also leads to increased learning.

Networks further help to avoid the so-called "brain-drain" better than other forms of organization by achieving a more structured retention of the people's knowledge within the company, even after they have left. Finally they can be an advantage in recruiting and retaining people, since the social web that develops around them can make people feel more at ease within the company.

Overall, networks are interactive, mobilizing, participative, spirited, and fun. They coordinate individual knowledge, accelerate its aggregation, and increase the effectiveness of its management. Also networks can be regarded as superior, in certain situations, because they:

- draw on specialized, yet complementary partner contributions, which extend the resource base and capabilities and entail production cost advantages,
- lead to improved co-ordination and control, through recurrent exchange relations, high degrees and scopes of information exchange, reciprocal obligations and periodic joint decision-making,
- create stronger performance incentives (economizing on co-ordination costs) through the matching of distribution of influence on the one hand, and of risks and rewards on the other.

Networks thus combine specialized efficiency, autonomous operating effectiveness, and asset-transferring capabilities.

Key Disadvantages of Networks. Networks do also have disadvantages. First, they may not have a particular reputation within the company because of the inherent difficulty to accurately judge the networks' actual performance. Thus they are sometimes not readily accepted by senior management.

Furthermore, they are harder to keep alive and to retain than other forms of organizing people, since they need continuous attention.

Another danger is that networks could become exclusive and not let the relevant people take part, thus becoming "cliquey" and self-serving. This can result in a limited scope of thinking and a certain path of dependency, thus inhibiting innovative ideas. This could have a serious detrimental effect, especially if a network is very powerful within the company. In addition, the collective knowledge of networks might be difficult to capture in some cases.

4.3 Knowledge Network Reference Types

Knowledge Network

> *"Each of the conversion modes can be understood as processes of self-transcendence, as every conversion involves transcending the self of individuals, teams or organizations." (Nonaka et al., 1998)*

As already mentioned, we distinguish categories of knowledge networks according to their underlying knowledge operational task. This refers to Nonaka and Konno (1998) and the SECI model, which describes the processes of socialization, externalization, combination, and internalization as four conversion modes from implicit to explicit knowledge.

Socialization involves the exchange of implicit knowledge between individuals in order to convey personal knowledge and experience. Joint experience results in new, shared implicit knowledge such as common values or technical skills. In practice, this could mean, for example, gaining intuitive and personal knowledge through physical proximity and directly communicating with customers or a supplier.

Externalization describes another transformation process. On the one hand the conversion of implicit knowledge into explicit knowledge and on the other, the exchange of knowledge between individuals and a group. Since implicit knowledge is difficult to express, the conversion process is often supported by the use of metaphors, analogies, stories, and language rich in imagery, as well as visualization aids, such as models, diagrams, or prototypes. In order to stage a constructive discussion and reach creative conclusions, a deductive or inductive mode of argumentation is also important.

Combination involves the transformation of explicit knowledge into more complex and more systematized explicit knowledge (Nonaka (1999) renamed this stage systematization). It is necessary to combine different fields of explicit knowledge with each other and make new knowledge available on an organization-wide basis. The systematization and refinement increases the practical value of existing knowledge and increases its transferability to all organizational units.

Internalization comprises the conversion of organization-wide, explicit knowledge into the implicit knowledge of the individual. This requires that the individual is able to recognize personally relevant knowledge within the organization. Continuous learning and the gathering of one's own experience through "learning-by-doing" may support employees in these internalization processes. In this way, capabilities and skills ("know-how") as well as firm visions and guidelines, may be internalized and thus shared throughout the whole company. This implicit knowledge and the experience gained on an individual level can be shared again through socialization-processes between individuals, so that the knowledge spiral may be set in motion once more.

When cultivating the relationships that are the basis for these knowledge operational tasks the transformational effects that information and communication technology can have on the form and intensity of communication, cooperation, and coordination need to be taken into account. The concept of "ba" (Nonaka and Konno, 1998) is a step into the right direction, but it is not yet a comprehensive view of how new media affects these processes.

It is important to further note here that in all these exchange processes new knowledge is created (Nonaka and Konno, 1998). To create new knowledge the knowledge work processes of locating, capturing, transferring, and sharing have to take place.

4.3.1 Derivation of Knowledge Network Reference Types

Referring to Nonaka's SECI model and the concept of "ba", we identified four knowledge network reference types, each pursuing a main transformation process, i.e., knowledge operational task. For example, in a knowledge network where explicit knowledge is primarily exchanged, the main knowledge operational task is the transformation from explicit into re-systematized explicit knowledge.

In order for implicit knowledge to be exchanged, as in the knowledge network reference type "experiencing", it first needs to be identified and then internalized through adaptation and model-learning.

The knowledge network reference type "materializing", in turn, deals with the process of identifying implicit knowledge, with its transformation into explicit knowledge being defined by concept and model learning and by the exchange of this explicit knowledge.

The knowledge network reference type "resystematizing" focuses on the identification of already available explicit knowledge that is interconnected and used for decision making, hence (re-)organized, and then distributed.

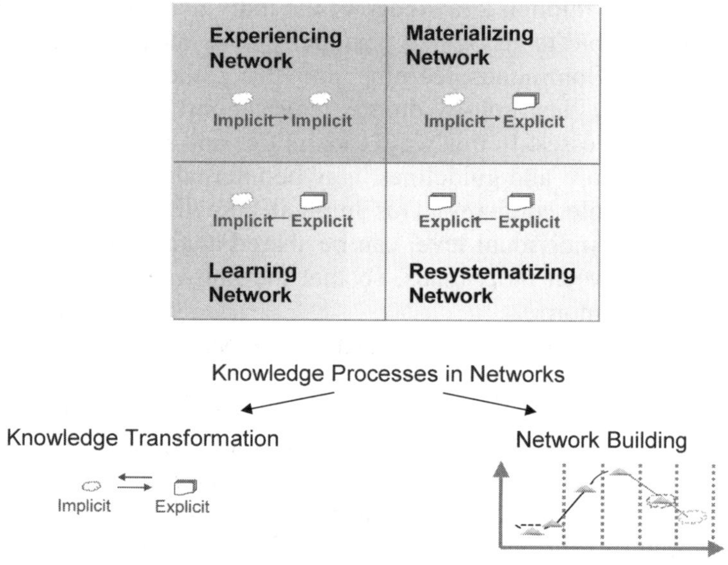

Fig. 5. Derivation of knowledge network reference types

Finally, the knowledge network reference type "learning" can be thought of as a network dealing with the identification of explicit knowledge and its internalization in order to apply it in actual circumstances.

As research has shown, knowledge transformation processes are at the center of knowledge networks. In order to meet the objecticves of the business processes and to support specific knowledge processes efficiently, appropriate facilitating conditions and tools have to be in place. This means that knowledge work processes, knowledge network architecture, and facilitating conditions have to mesh. Knowledge network reference types can be used to identify "ideal" forms and arrangements in order to contribute to specific business goals.

Building on the model of structuration theory, an additional aspect has to be taken into account when setting up a knowledge network. Management should not only focus on how to support the generic knowledge processes, meaning the interactive transformation of implicit and explicit knowledge (knowledge transformation), but also on network building, i.e., the life-cycle of the network.

Layers of a Knowledge Network Reference Type

The initial framework of knowledge networks encompasses the following elements:

- *Actors* as individuals, groups, organizations.
- *Relationships between actors* which can be categorized by form, content and intensity.
- *Resources* which may be used by actors to network with other individuals, groups or organizations.
- *Organizational properties*, including structural and cultural dimensions such as control mechanisms, standard operating-procedures, norms and values, communication patterns, etc.

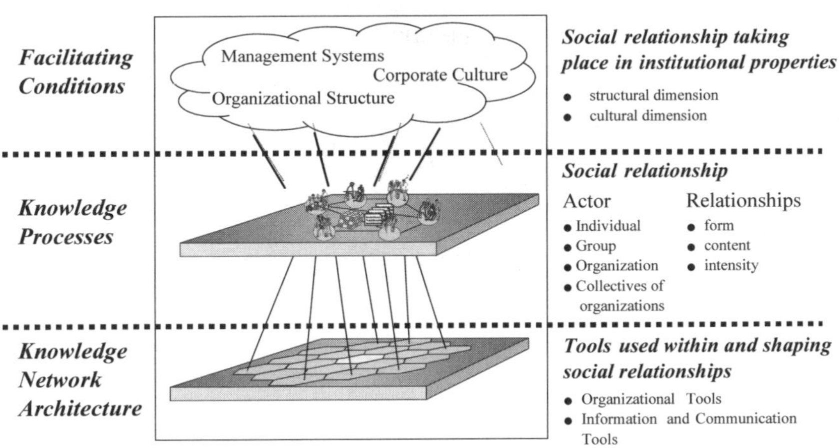

Fig. 6. Layers of a knowledge network

These components can be perceived as either static (short-term perspective) or dynamic (long-term perspective). From a micro perspective, we conceptualize knowledge networks on the following three building blocks:

(a) facilitating conditions, (b) knowledge work processes and (c) knowledge network architecture which we will describe in the following.

Knowledge Work Processes

In our framework we defined knowledge work processes in the main categories; locating and capturing knowledge, transferring and sharing knowledge, and knowledge creation. The bottom line for all categories is the application of existing or newly gained knowledge to create value. As knowledge should not be managed per se, but needs also to be tightly connected to business drivers, the application of knowledge is at the center of all knowledge management activities.

Most companies start with focusing on the knowledge they have and on the content of this knowledge. In this phase, knowledge management is mostly about locating and capturing knowledge. Over time, companies start to focus more on new processes that enable them to share knowledge across units and to create completely new knowledge assets. This phase is the knowledge transfer phase. Finally, the most ambitious and challenging phase, knowledge creation takes place. Some scholars predict that within ten years knowledge creation will be the key factor distinguishing successful companies from less successful ones.

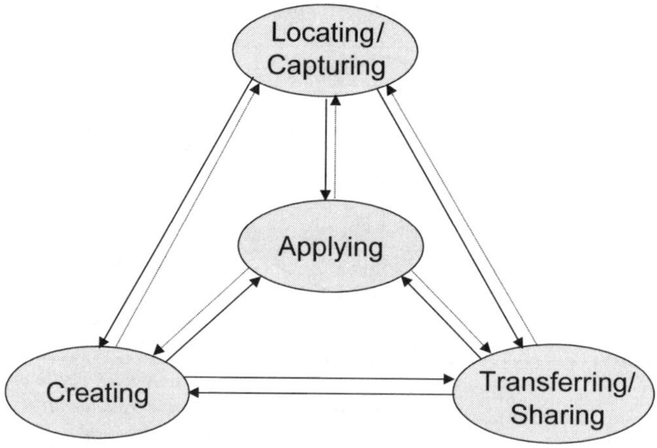

Fig. 7. Knowledge work processes

The following figure demonstrates the evolution of knowledge work processes:

A Model of Company Development

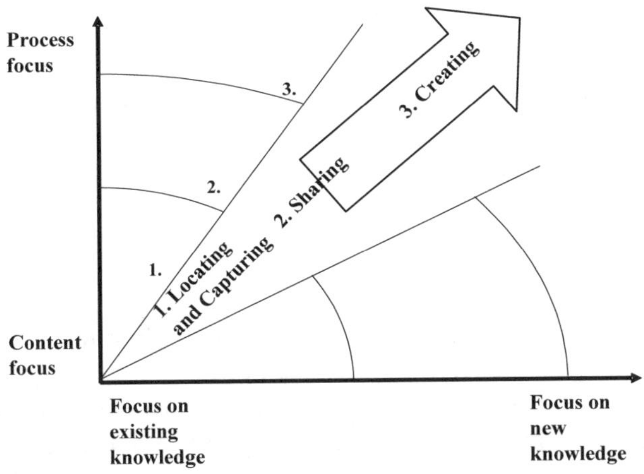

Fig. 8. Evolution of knowledge work processes

Knowledge Locating/Capturing

In order to locate and capture existing knowledge many companies develop "knowledge maps" and "yellow pages."

Profile **Arthur Andersen**

At Arthur Andersen, for example, "yellow pages" allow the organization to search for specific skill categories and to identify the person who truly holds the needed knowledge. Such "yellow pages" are greatly reducing research costs.

There are also more sophisticated systems such as a "task profiling system", which specifies the task at hand and thus increases efficiency.

Profile **Microsoft**

When a project manager at Microsoft starts a new product development project, he/she specifies the task at hand. There is no actual search for skills. The aim is rather to specify the task as accurately as possible. Once the task has been specified and articulated, the system starts to search through the skill categories and comes up with the best people available. Still, the main weakness of these systems is that they often neglect implicit knowledge. A large part of the knowledge people have is of implicit nature. It is almost impossible to design a system where the search categories truly match with the great variation of implicit knowledge at hand.

This example signifies the need for the second step a company has to take in order to locate and capture knowledge. This would be making implicit knowledge accessible throughout the organization.

Profile **HP**

Since only the holders themselves can express implicit knowledge, HP has created the Connex system. Each employee has his or her own homepage. The headline of that homepage is "What can I do for you?" It is a selling homepage that is not based on skill categories. Everybody tries to describe his or her skills in more of an essay format that could actually be of use to everyone in the company.

Knowledge Sharing/Transferring

The ability to create knowledge and move it from one part of the organization to another is a basis for competitive advantage (Grant, 1996; Inkpen, 1996). Also, it is realized that "an enormous amount of information and knowledge resides in the minds and electronic mail of key people, but this material is rarely organized in a way that allows its transmission to others" (Powell, 1998, p. 237). Regarding sharing and transferring knowledge within companies, the efficient use and leverage of existing knowledge, as well as the capability to work with knowledge tasks, leads to cost reducetions and increases in efficiency by shortening reaction times and avoiding re-inventing the wheel (Anthes, 1998; von Krogh and Köhne, 1998).

Knowledge sharing/transferring can be defined as the exchange of knowledge (implicit and/or explicit) between individuals, groups, and departments both within and outside a company. Sharing/transferring of cognitive frames of reference and capabilities can be used for accomplishing a task and enables a shared interpretation and coordinated action (Kriwet, 1997; Nonaka and Takeuchi, 1995; Probst et al., 1999; von Krogh and Köhne, 1998). It takes place when the recipient has gained a primarily similar understanding as the source (Haerem et al., 1996). It may happen consciously and purposefully, as well as accidentally and unsystematically

(Davenport and Prusak, 1998; Hamel et al., 1989; Inkpen and Crossan, 1995).

Knowledge sharing/transferring takes place in three phases: initiation and coordination, translation and negotiation, and integration (von Krogh and Köhne, 1998), as shown in the following figure:

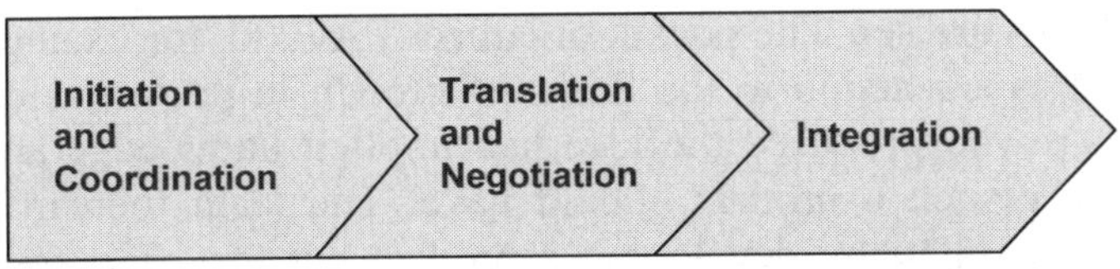

Fig. 9. Phases of the process of sharing/transferring knowledge

These three phases do not always have to follow sequentially: steps back into previous phases are likely and several knowledge flows of a transfer on a larger scale could be in different phases (von Krogh and Köhne, 1998). Besides, as time passes by, a new or changed need for knowledge flows may evolve, causing the orientation of the knowledge sharing/transferring activities to shift and adapt. For these reasons, knowledge sharing/transferring is not an easy task and is limited in its manageability.

Knowledge Creation

Companies create knowledge by enlarging either their explicit knowledge or their implicit knowledge. Enlarging explicit knowledge can be accomplished by transforming existing implicit knowledge into explicit knowledge. This is one of the greatest challenges of knowledge management.

Profile **ABB**

ABB introduced a customer focus program. This program uncovered that only 20% of all customer complaints regarding the technologies were fed back to the engineers. This implies that 80% of all complaints were kept implicit among field-representatives. With the customer focus program a feedback loop was installed. Through this program, the implicit knowledge could be made explicit and was fed back to the engineers, thus enlarging the explicit knowledge base of the company.

As the following example illustrates, a product idea is very often based on implicit knowledge and will not always surface, unless there are certain mechanisms in place to make that knowledge explicit.

Profile **Sharp**

Sharp organizes "urgent project teams" in which any employee can propose a product development project. If top management is convinced, resources are made available and timelines and product development goals are set. The pocket organizer PA7000, for example, was developed as a reaction to the limits of growth in pocket calculators. The person who proposed the idea had implicit knowledge about the functionality such a product should have. The team then made this knowledge explicit by developing a product concept. The result was one of the best selling items in the history of Sharp.

Enlarging the implicit knowledge base of the company also enhances knowledge creation.

Profile **Eisai**

In order to understand the enlargement of the implicit knowledge base within a company, the already introduced example of the company Eisai can be used. Through the "Preceptorship Program" mentioned above, the managers gained insights that enlarged the implicit knowledge base of the company.

Knowledge networks are predominantly used to transfer and share existing and/or new knowledge. Sixty-one percent (61%) considered this knowledge working process as the most important one in the network, followed by creating (16%), capturing (9%), applying and locating (7%). The domination of sharing and transferring processes could be interpreted by the visibility of their output and their ease of use.
Our empirical research (Enkel and Wicki, 2002) showed that within all the network types all knowledge work processes could be found to a similar extent. This equal distribution occurred in small, as well as in large networks.

4.3.2 Facilitating Conditions

Facilitating conditions are the environment in which the knowledge network operations take place. They can enable or hinder the knowledge operational task. As research has shown, one can distinguish between facilitating conditions within a particular knowledge network (internal) and those surrounding the network (external). We argue that when setting up a network external company-related facilitating conditions are pre-given, and thus cannot be influenced by the network itself. Nevertheless they can support or hinder the set up of a network. On the other hand, facilitating conditions within the network can be influenced, both directly and indirectly.

Company-related Facilitating Conditions

As for example, the communication style, the organizational form, the management systems in place, the incentives given by the company, and the measurement of the company's successes, can influence the performance of the network and can be considered facilitating conditions. Since the knowledge network can, in the long run, influence the culture of the company, a reciprocal relationship is in effect.

Network-related Facilitating Conditions

The facilitating conditions of the network itself are derived from the characteristics of a network. We distinguish between structural facilitating conditions on the network level, i.e. network issues, such as the size of the network or particular skills represented, and cultural facilitating conditions, such as values and value affecting/value-related issues (Köhne et al., 2000).

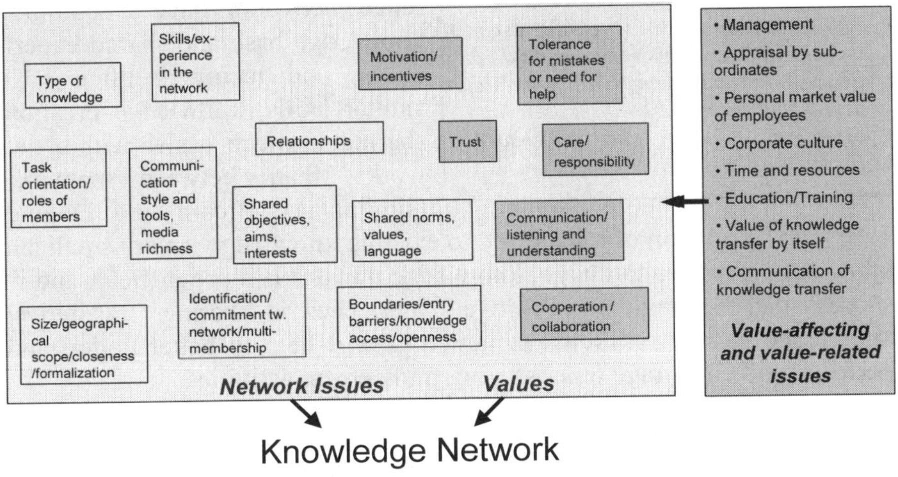

Fig. 10. Facilitating conditions

For each knowledge network reference type, these facilitating conditions have to be in place to a certain extent. However, if facilitating conditions are not properly and satisfactorily in place, using certain tools can influence them. While structural facilitating conditions can be influenced directly cultural facilitating conditions can only be influenced indirectly. The following provides an overview of the facilitating conditions identified in our research.

Network Issues

Type of Knowledge. Regarding knowledge work processes, the type of knowledge – whether explicit or implicit – plays a key role, since explicit knowledge is more schematic and easier to transfer systematically than implicit knowledge (Lam, 1997; Nonaka, 1992). Therefore, if different networks base their knowledge and their use of knowledge on different types of knowledge (e.g. one network is based more on explicit and another is based more on implicit knowledge), knowledge sharing/transferring is much more difficult (Lam, 1997). Also, implicit knowledge, which is embedded in networks, might be quite difficult to transfer/share among networks (Wenger, 1998a).

Skills and Experience in the Network. Existing skills and experiences are very significant in the knowledge sharing/transfer process. This is because the ability to perceive and to assimilate transferred knowledge depends strongly on the correlation of transferred knowledge and existing skills and knowledge and experiences (Cohen and Levinthal, 1990).

> *"If the receptor knows very little, he can do very little even with the simple data, because he cannot generate the mass of detail that is required to put it into execution." (Gomory, cited in Leonard-Barton, 1995).*

Since networks have a common knowledge base and shared experiences, and members often have similar skills, knowledge creation/sharing is much easier within networks than between networks (similar see Brown and Duguid, 1998). If the relation of transferred to existing knowledge is very small and knowledge gaps are too large, knowledge transfer is more difficult and its success can be hindered. Positive experiences in sharing/ transferring knowledge within and between networks will help to better understand, perform, and encourage other sharing/transferring activities.

Task Orientation/Roles of Members in the Network. A high task orientation is hindering and complicates knowledge work processes. In any case, extending role definitions by defining knowledge creation/sharing explicitly as a task and promoting such knowledge tasks as enrichment for networks, will, in the end, support knowledge work processes.

Relationships. Poor relationships within and between networks hinder or complicate knowledge creation/sharing activities, whereas positive relationships – which are built for example on trust – favor these activities. Once relationships are established, they help people understand and learn about the needs and the behaviors of others and therefore may better ensure that adequate knowledge is created/shared (Szulanski, 1994).

Communication Style, Tools, and Media Richness. Within networks, specific communication styles exist and members know best how to communicate and to share/transfer knowledge (Wenger, 1998b). If communication styles or tools of different networks vary too much and if adaptation to other communication styles and tools is too difficult, knowledge sharing/transferring between networks may prove more difficult. Another aspect regarding communication is media richness. This concerns the use of various and complementary media and has a positive impact on sharing/transferring activities within and between networks (Wathne et al., 1996).

Shared Norms, Values, and Language. Knowledge work processes within a network are supported by similar understandings, similar norms and values, and similar behaviors and communication patterns that exist in the network (Brown and Duguid, 1998; Davenport and Prusak, 1998; Wenger, 1998a, 1998b; Zucker and Schmitz, 1994). Regarding knowledge creation/sharing between networks, the aforementioned aspects (norms, values, etc) can vary enough so that knowledge activities between networks may be complicated (also Kogut and Zander, 1993). Also, finding a common language will have a positive impact for knowledge creation/sharing among different networks (Davenport and Prusak, 1998).

Shared Objectives, Aims, Interests. When shared objectives, aims, and interests in networks are in tandem with knowledge creation/sharing objectives and activities, these shared objectives will support knowledge processes within networks. But, when a knowledge project is introduced in which networks/network members perceive a conflict of objectives, the motivation for knowledge creation/sharing might dwindle, and the knowledge transfer project may be unsuccessful or not even carried out.

Identification/Commitment of the Members towards the Network/ Membership in Other Networks. Identification and commitment of members towards their "own" network support knowledge creation/

sharing within networks. However, if this identification and commitment is too strong and narrowly focused, so that no attention is given to other networks, then no knowledge creation/ sharing between networks may occur, since network members develop some sort of "tunnel vision". A balance of knowledge creation/sharing among networks can be achieved if people belong to more than on network (i.e. boundary spanners). Thereby, knowledge creation/sharing is facilitated because they can connect to different networks by understanding their needs, interests and backgrounds; they can help to evaluate knowledge in different networks; they can "translate" the knowledge of different networks and make it understandable to others; and they can "transport" and propagate knowledge between and in different networks (Powell, 1998; Wenger, 1998b).

Boundaries of Networks/Entry Barriers/Knowledge Access/Openness. Openness of networks/network members – the willingness to openly communicate and not hide information, motivations, etc - has a positive impact and is an essential value for knowledge creation/sharing within and between networks (similar von Krogh and Köhne, 1998). Therefore open boundaries of networks can facilitate creation/sharing activities between networks, while closed boundaries are hindering them.

Size, Geographical Scope/Proximity/Formalization of Networks. The size of a network influences knowledge creation/sharing activities, so that larger networks need more impersonal and more formalized communication tools and methods, whereas in smaller networks more personal and informal activities are appropriate. Also, if a geographically dispersed network does not have enough shared information and no common language, knowledge transferring/sharing is more difficult to carry out, and most likely reduced to a great extent. Local proximity of networks/network members, in turn, has a positive effect on knowledge work processes within and between networks (von Krogh and Köhne, 1998).

Values. "Values are filters by which we make decisions" (Ellis and Hall, 1994). The quality of values therefore has a general effect on knowledge creation and transfer. If there is a lack of understanding of these value filters, and/or the value filters do not complement each other, miscommunication and conflict within the organization will arise. If one speaks about the function of values as filters, the different types of boundaries and levels within an organization have an essential role to play. The boundaries and levels within an organization can be determined through different core values of organizational units, groups, etc. These value-induced filtering mechanisms on the boundaries between levels and also networks, can lead to restrict the flow of information between different organizational units, organizational levels, as well as different networks within the organization (similar Hall, 1995).

Communication, Listening, and Understanding. Successful communication is essential in order to support knowledge transfer. On the one hand, communication can be seen as a prerequisite for cooperation and collaboration. On the other hand, in order to communicate successfully, it is also important to establish other relevant values for knowledge transfer such as trust, responsibility, etc. Important elements of successful communication that particularly influence knowledge transfer are listening and understanding. Effective and active listening is a requirement for understanding one another. If the communication patterns of the people involved deviate from each other, active listening has an essential role to play. In this case, it is absolutely necessary to find out if the misunderstanding is a result of different communication patterns. Further, to transfer knowledge effectively a context of understanding must be created (Dove, 1996). Common patterns of understanding help to integrate new information. Consequently, listening and understanding have a positive impact on knowledge creation/sharing.

Cooperation/Collaboration. Cooperation and collaboration are important values to support knowledge work processes, for they recognize the needs regarding knowledge creation/sharing. A high level of cooperation and collaboration often helps to establish a "common ground" (e.g. language, culture) for knowledge processes (Davenport and Prusak, 1998). Cooperation and collaboration also have an influence on other values (e.g. trust).

Trust. Trust can be defined as an optimistic expectation during a common task, in which the trusting party has something at stake, and has no control over the other party. This can be adapted for the situation of knowledge creation/sharing between two people. If there is a lack of trust, it will lead to negative effects on knowledge work processes (e.g. information hiding, questioning of transferred information) (Davenport and Prusak, 1998).

Care/Responsibility. Personally caring also supports knowledge creation/sharing. Caring includes being responsible for new information, preparing sufficiently for a knowledge process, ensuring the quality of information, etc. A high degree of personal responsibility, not only for the own work, but also for the company as a whole and for the issues of knowledge creation/sharing, are important values for supporting knowledge transfer (Lloyd, 1998; Process Edge Technologies, 1998). Responsibility and care are values that may help to avoid the "not-invented-here" syndrome.

Tolerance for Mistakes or Need for Help. The permission to make mistakes and to ask for help without negative consequences can also support knowledge work processes (Davenport and Prusak, 1998). If people are afraid of committing an error, it is very likely that they will not share their knowledge until they rate their work absolutely acceptable. If asking for help is undesirable, an obstacle to integrate transferred knowledge is created.

Value-related Issues. In order to implement knowledge management activities in the company, cultural issues must be considered. This includes specific values which support the demands concerning the management of knowledge. The values of a knowledge culture often go against established hierarchy and control. On a deeper level, a profound conflict between the principles and values of the hierarchy, and the knowledge culture, may arise. Understanding the knowledge culture and its values is one of the first and most important steps of successful knowledge management.

Profile **Skandia**

Skandia is a Swedish insurance and financial services group that has grown faster than Microsoft since 1991. From 1988 to 1993 Skandia implemented a reporting system that allowed them to locate and measure the value of their knowledge. They also implemented a customer database which gave insurance salesmen a direct access to information about every single customer, thereby enabling them to design the right product-mix for the customer. From 1993 to 1998 Skandia started to focus on a high trust culture that would foster knowledge sharing. They stated very explicit values and introduced training programs that enhanced these values. Skandia also founded an international expansion unit. This unit accumulated knowledge about all aspects of internalization, captured this knowledge in manuals and developed teaching programs to leverage this knowledge. The result was a major time reduction in establishing new groups abroad (Bukowitz and Williams, 1999).

The following components which influence those values and/or stand in relation to them are also part of the model:

Value of Knowledge Creation/Transfer by Itself. The literature on the subject of "human values" states that values are closely related to the success of the enterprise. Therefore, it is essential that a company defines its values accurately and also combines them with the business strategy (Botero, 1995; Hart, 1995). What does this mean for knowledge creation/transfer? It is obvious that knowledge work processes have to be of certain value for the company. It must be emphasized that knowledge transfer has a positive impact. If the value of knowledge creation/sharing for the company is relatively high, clearly defined, linked to competitive strategy, and matched with the values of individuals, a positive impact on creation/sharing knowledge will surface.

Culture. An established knowledge culture (e.g. shared values about how to collaborate and to create and share knowledge) facilitates the creation/ sharing of knowledge. However, diverse sub-cultures and varying ways of dealing with knowledge make knowledge creation/sharing more difficult (Davenport and Prusak, 1998).

Communication of Knowledge Transfer. The relevant issues of a knowledge project need to be properly and accurately communicated to the participants. Goal, purpose, and value of a knowledge transfer must be articulated. This type of communication can prepare people for new information and therefore have a positive impact (Dove, 1996).

Time and Resources. If knowledge creation/sharing is acknowledged as valuable, appropriate time and resources for knowledge transfer activities should be provided. Since knowledge transfer is a time and resource consuming process, a lack of time/resources has a negative impact on a knowledge project (Davenport and Prusak, 1998). Therefore, time and resources for knowledge creation/sharing have to be provided.

Management. The activities of management in order to support knowledge creation/transfer can be very diverse. For example, management can serve as a model for knowledge transfer activities by continuously sharing the status of knowledge activities taking place within the company and acknowledging those employees involved.

Appraisal. The appraisal systems of the company have to consider knowledge transfer explicitly to show employees that knowledge transfer has value for the company (KPMG Germany, 1999). Appraisal has an impact on motivation and therefore on knowledge creation/sharing. For this reason, appraisal systems have to include the appraisal of knowledge management activities to encourage motivation.

Motivation/Incentives. Values and incentives have an effect on motivation. To motivate employees, incentive and motivation systems have to reward knowledge activities (KPMG Germany, 1999). Knowledge creation/sharing must be perceived as worthwhile and attractive to encourage people to share knowledge. Intrinsic motivation depends strongly on personal values. The impact of intrinsic motivation on knowledge work processes can be both negative (e.g. "knowledge is power") and positive (e.g. "knowledge sharing is power"). If the employees internalize the value knowledge sharing has for them, they can be motivated intrinsically. Extrinsic motivation (e.g. incentives) can also have a positive impact on knowledge creation/transfer.

As empirical research has shown (Enkel and Wicki, 2002), when dealing with both, small and large networks, different types of facilitating conditions become relevant. In large knowledge networks there are many factors restraining the networks to purse their tasks efficiently. The predominant reason is conflicting goals (19%), followed by lack of trust (14%), and lack of experience with other actors (12%). Geographical distances (6%), coalition building within the network (6%), and new definitions of business processes due to network activities (2%) are present, but of less importance. However, in small networks, facilitating conditions such as geographical distances (13%), lingual and cultural problems (13%), and conflicting goals (11%), are the most significant, while coalition building (1%), lack of experience with other actors (4%), and the new definition of business processes due to network activities (4%) are of less importance.

Personal Market Value of Employees. Sharing and transferring knowledge often raises the question: What about my unique value? A negative impact on knowledge work processes can be that individual excellence is highly regarded in most companies and, frequently, the only focus of reward (McDermott, 1995). Knowledge management and on-the-job learning can help to develop the "personal market value" of employees. This must be instilled as a value within the knowledge culture of the company. Believing that one is "raising their own personal market value" when sharing knowledge can be seen as a form of intrinsic motivation, explaining why it has a positive impact on knowledge creation/sharing.

Education/Training. Education/training can be seen as an important part of the human value system, because values can be transmitted through education/training. Adequate education and training in "knowledge working" and the herewith-intended transmission of the "values of a knowledge culture" (Process Edge Technologies, 1998) have a positive impact on transferring knowledge.

4.3.3 Knowledge Network Architecture

> *"Man is a tool-using animal ... without tools he is nothing, with tools he is all" (Thomas Carlyle, essayist & historian, in Ruggles, 1997).*

This chapter describes in more detail the knowledge network architecture layer. According to our research framework, we classify and describe information and communication tools (ICT), as well as organizational tools and methods, and their potential to support knowledge networks.

Before discussing the knowledge network architecture layer, it seems to be useful to explain the role and the "essence" of tools, as well as our understanding of tools.

In the context of knowledge networks tools are of great relevance, since without them a knowledge network cannot function properly and successfully.

Unfortunately the question of which tools to employ is not easy to answer, given that even though the appropriate tool is being used, it is not always the case that it is being used properly. In the realm of knowledge management this has prompted a very polarized discussion about the usefulness of tools, especially ICT tools. Vendors and producers of ICT tools continually praise the nearly unlimited possibilities of their software products. Nevertheless, for many different reasons these tools often do not deliver what they promise. One reason for failure in practice may be that the wrong tools have been selected. This reason however, forces a company to go back and re-assess their selection criteria and process. Another reason is that the impact of tools on the organization has not been reflected and appropriately measured. Also, one should remember that human beings are the "users" of these tools. These users may often not know how to use them, may not have the correct skills to use them, may not fully understand why they are being used in the first place, or they simply do not like the tools and refuse to work with them. In short, users are an unpredictable variable, and as members of knowledge networks they should not be neglected when issues of tool support or ICT system design are discussed.

The aforementioned can commonly be observed in companies. One could thus conclude that the main pitfall in knowledge management is that tools are selected without a proper assessment and are not used correctly. Regarding tool utilization, the notion of "less often is more" has also been confirmed in a bilateral project: "A knowledge network or community should make a decision for at least one ICT tool in order to share and transfer knowledge globally." (DaimlerChrysler, 2000).

Our understanding of tools will now be discussed, so as to avoid any complications described above. Initially, to support knowledge networks tools should be defined not just as technologies (e.g. Ruggles, 1997), but rather as ICT and organizational tools. Both ICT tools and organizational tools should be employed simultaneously in order to support the performance of knowledge networks. With this definition two things are implied. First, we argue that not every situation occurring in knowledge networks can be solved with ICT alone. Knowledge networks need organizational tools as well to work successfully. Second, ensuring that the tools were selected and used properly, both the ICT and organizational tools require integration, as the following figure illustrates.

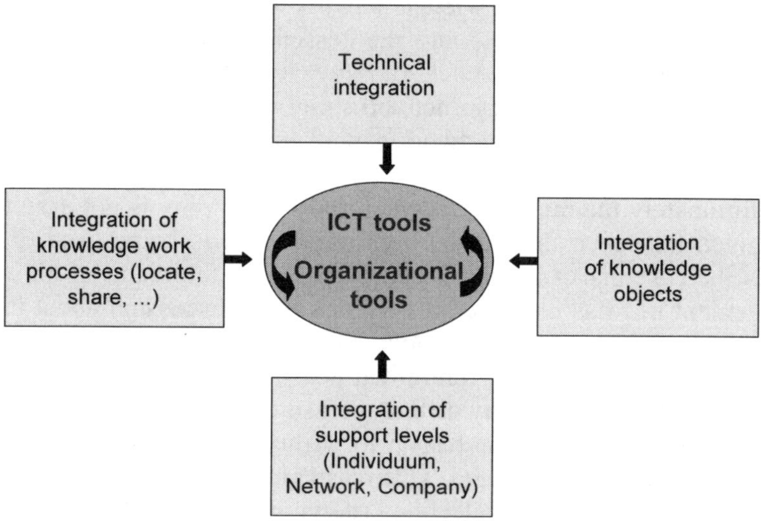

Fig. 11. Requirements for a knowledge network architecture

One problem associated with an integrated approach, as with other interdisciplinary knowledge management approaches, is that it is rather complex. Therefore, the danger exists that statements regarding knowledge networks and their support tools may be too generic and superficial to be genuinely useful.

Also important, ICT tools often have completely different characteristics than organizational tools. Therefore, ICT-based processes in knowledge networks quite often have to be designed in conjunction with organizational tools. For example, a virtual community which is exclusively based on ICT systems needs other forms of support and incentives associated with more traditional forms of knowledge networks (for design of incentive systems in virtual communities see e.g. Kim, 2000).

Furthermore, the usage of ICT fundamentally changes the quality of the collaboration in knowledge networks. For example, ICT-based communication has a completely different quality, good or bad depending on the situation, than personal, face-to-face communication. For instance, trust in social relationships may be very difficult to establish via ICT. Therefore, in knowledge networks organizational tools cannot be directly compared with ICT tools (see Eberle, 2000) in the field of learning technologies.

A first step should be to develop a classification scheme for both organizational and ICT tools. Such an integrative classification framework is described in the following paragraph.

Tool Classification Framework

Since most classification schemes fit either for ICT tools (see e.g. Lehner, 2000) or for organizational tools (see e.g. Czichos, 1990; Skyrme, 1999; Staehle, 1999), but not for both, we have developed our own integrative classification model for organizational and ICT tools, which comprises the following main tool classes (see figure below).

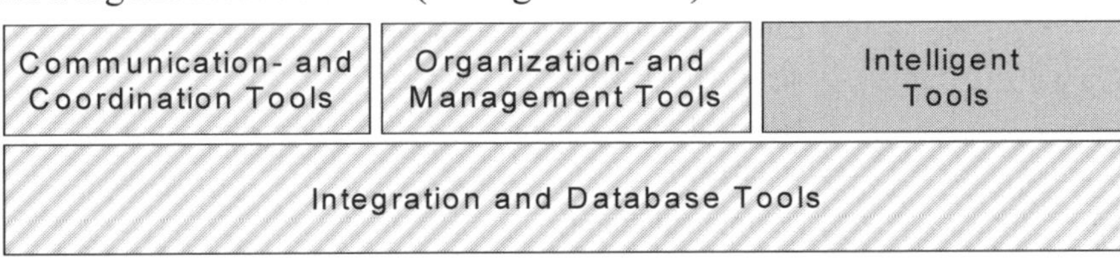

Fig. 12. Classification model for ICT and organizational tools

Communication and Coordination Tools. This main tool class is comprised of ICT tools and organizational tools, which can be used in order to support communication and coordination in knowledge networks.

Table 1. Communication and coordination tools

Organizational tools	Knowledge forums Think tank Knowledge workshops Coffee corners/talk rooms Meeting and moderation tools Conversation and negotiation techniques Active listening Language tools (dialog, story telling, common language, metaphors, controlled vocabulary, organizational thesaurus and dictionary)
ICT tools	Document management/archiving Workflow management Messaging/e-mail Calendaring/scheduling Group decision support systems Real-time conferencing systems (video conferencing, audio conferencing, data conferencing (chat, white-board, application sharing)) Non-real-time conferencing systems (e.g. discussion databases) Learning platforms Group editing/group document handling Community tools Collaborative filtering CSCW-suites

ICT tools within this main tool class are various types of groupware tools (a corresponding term is Computer Supported Cooperative Work (CSCW)), which explicitly address the issues of communication and coordination (Lotus, 1999).

Organizational tools that support communication and coordination in knowledge networks are knowledge forums, think tanks, knowledge workshops, coffee corners/talk rooms, meeting and moderation tools, conversation and negotiation techniques, as well as different language tools.

Organization and Management Tools. A large number of organizational and ICT tools can be used to support organization and management of knowledge networks. Tools in this category can be used not only to manage and control knowledge networks, but also for visualizing, structuring and (re-)systematizing issues in knowledge networks.

Table 2. Organizational and management tools

Organizational tools	Management tools: Performance management tools Motivation tools Creativity tools Problem solving tools Planning tools Self management tools Conflict management tools Learning tools Knowledge vision/goals Rewards and incentives Organizational structure tools: Group work Project management Space management Knowledge units Roles and responsibilities Organizational culture tools: Change agent Corporate culture change programs Organizational development tools
ICT tools	Personal information management (PIM) Decision support systems (DSS), management and executive information systems (MIS/EIS) Simulation and modeling tools Visualization tools Creativity tools Measuring tools

Organizational tools within this class can be further divided into management tools, organizational structure tools and organizational culture tools. On the ICT side we also identified a broad range of software to support organizational and management aspects in knowledge networks. Table 2 provides an overview of organizational and ICT tools that support organization and management in knowledge networks.

Integration and Database Tools. Integration is an important topic for knowledge management and in particular for knowledge networks. Integration comprises technical as well as organizational aspects such as the integration of technology, knowledge work processes, knowledge objects (implicit and explicit knowledge), and support levels (individual, network, company).

Organizational integration tools encompass an integration action plan or an integration matrix (Czichos, 1990). For ICT, there exists a large range of tools that can be used for integration purposes. Tool suites for example offer specific possibilities to build an overall ICT infrastructure, covering all knowledge work processes. Such integration tools are i-net-technologies, CSCW/groupware suites, knowledge management suites, and enterprise portals. We also see database tools in this category since databases quite often play an important role within an integrated ICT environment. Table 3 provides an overview of integration and database tools.

Table 3. Integration and database tools

Organizational tools	Integration action plan Integration matrix
ICT tools	I-net-technologies (hypertext/-media, e-mail, search engines and catalogs, discussion- and news-groups, chat, yellow pages, expert maps, audio- and video-communication, database access (CGI, …)) Web-enabled applications (e.g. web-based document management or workflow management, enterprise portals, push technologies, video/audio-streaming) CSCW/groupware-suites Knowledge management suites Enterprise portals Databases, data dictionaries Repositories Data warehousing

Intelligent Tools. This tool class comprises ICT tools, which possess a certain degree of "intelligence".

Some emerge from the field of artificial intelligence, while others are called intelligent agents, or belong to the concept of "business intelligence" (BI). Since intelligent tools are an ICT-specific tool class, no organizational tools are listed here.

Table 4. Intelligent tools

ICT tools	Intelligent agents Data mining Text mining Skill mining Business intelligence Categorization/clustering tools, Problem solving tools (e.g. neural networks, reasoning, rule-based systems, intelligent knowledge bases, expert systems)

Particularities and Differences of ICT and Organizational Tools

As previously mentioned, ICT and organizational tools differ in many aspects. These differences cannot be ignored when using tools in knowledge networks. First, it is important to point out that ICT and organizational tools affect a knowledge network in different ways. For example, face-to-face communications in groups must follow other rules compared to communication via an online communication system. The moderation of traditional meetings requires other specific skills, than the moderation of a virtual discussion group. Each tool requires certain skills and appropriate conditions to use it successfully.

What is particularly true for organizational tools and for some ICT tools, is that they cannot be deployed short term in a knowledge network without further considerations. Organizational tools such as motivational tools, incentive systems, performance measurement tools, organizational culture tools, and other strategic management tools, have to consider the existing structural and cultural conditions within the company. The manner in which these tools are used is most often deeply rooted within the corporate culture of the company. This is an aspect why organizational tools cannot be dealt with in the same way as an ICT tool. Given the broadness of their effect and the sensitivity surrounding many organizational management and culture tools, these tools must be adapted carefully.

When discussing ICT tools, organizational culture is too often slighted or ignored entirely in academic studies and in practice, even though success of adopting new information system technology also depends on organizational culture (Klepper and Hoffman, 2000).

It is important for knowledge networks to gain influence within the company in order to receive support from management or other tool owners (e.g. the IT department or other company units), as the networks themselves are not necessarily tool owners. Generally, it is crucial to align different tools with each other for ultimate success.

To achieve this alignment and hence success, an ongoing dialogue between the knowledge network and the relevant people and interest groups (i.e. management, IT department, concerned business units, etc) is required.

Knowledge Network ICT Architecture Model

In the following we outline a knowledge network architecture model from an ICT perspective, integrating key functionalities to support knowledge networks (Raimann et al., 2000).

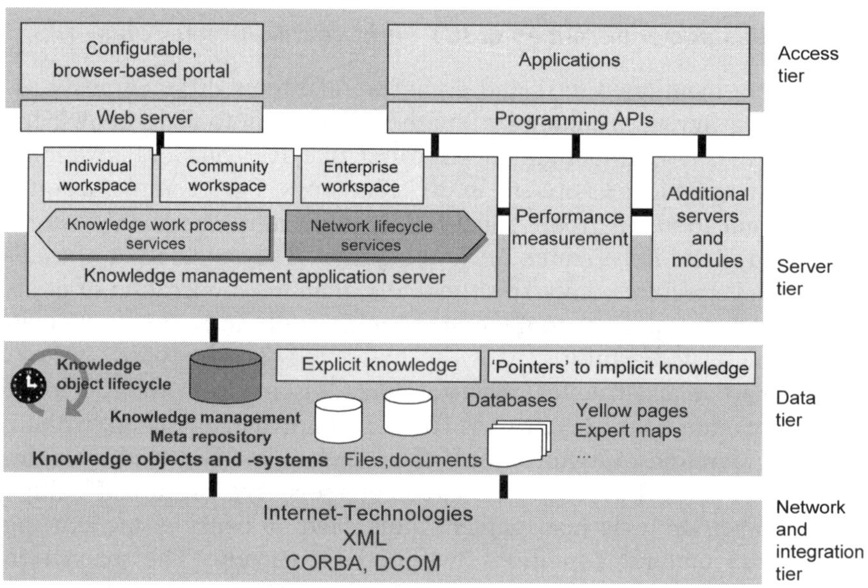

Fig. 13. Knowledge network ICT architecture

The architecture, from a functional point of view, is comprised of the following:

Basic Services to Support Knowledge Networks. As previously mentioned, two basic possibilities exist on how knowledge networks can be supported with ICT. The first possibility is to directly support the knowledge work process occurring in knowledge networks with so called knowledge work process services (Raimann et al., 2000). Supported knowledge work processes are locating/capturing and sharing/transferring of knowledge and, in particular, the creation of new knowledge (von Krogh, 1999).

The second possibility is network support systems from network lifecycle services that support the lifecycle of a network. For example, these services have to provide check-in/check-out mechanisms for the network members. Collaborative tools and functions are also important for network building. Additional services might be those which control the network and also help to visualize the network.

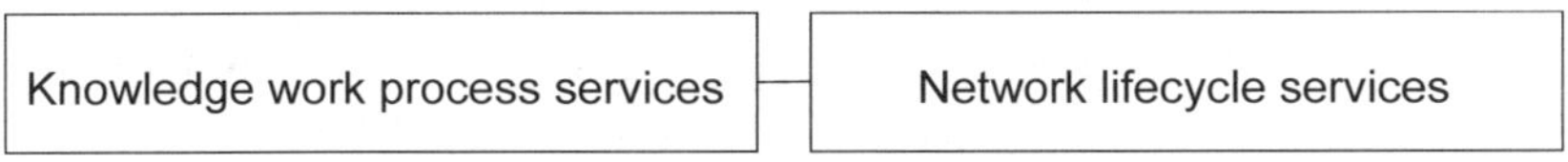

Fig. 14. Knowledge networks architecture - basic services

Provision of "Work Spaces". A knowledge network is embedded in an organization. Therefore the knowledge network architecture has to address individuals as network members, the network itself, and the surrounding organization, with appropriate services. In order to enable knowledge exchange between the different organizational levels, the architecture should provide different "work spaces" for the individual, network, and organization, which have to be connected with each other.

Knowledge Base. The knowledge base within a company-wide knowledge management architecture includes and integrates all types of explicit as well as ("pointers" to) implicit sources of knowledge and also different types of knowledge systems (e.g. ERP systems, groupware systems).

It is important to recognize that these knowledge objects are not static, but rather dynamic. This means that each knowledge object, starting with its creation, goes through a certain knowledge object lifecycle, in which it has a specific, well-defined state at every moment. This has to be considered when designing and implementing a knowledge network architecture.

A major implication of knowledge management is the efficient use of meta-information. It is used, for example, to categorize, define, and describe other data in order to deal with different contexts of knowledge. Examples are maps and data to unify the access to disparate data sources (GartnerGroup, 1999b). Meta-information is also used in order to manage the "dynamic" knowledge object lifecycle and to administrate user profile information, which is required for the realization of profile-based applications. Such meta-information is stored in a knowledge management meta-repository.

Performance Measurement. In order to be able to rate the success of knowledge networks, it is essential to evaluate the outcome of the knowledge management activities. Therefore functions to measure the network performance are required. IT-based knowledge networks need functionalities that visualize the results of the network usage, so that management can see the return on investment (Högberg and Edvinson, 1998).

A knowledge base can be a central element of a knowledge network measurement system. Many "online measures" are imaginable and can actually be implemented, such as evaluating the different knowledge work processes of building, sharing and applying knowledge (Raimann et al., 2000). With appropriate ICT tools, a "balanced scorecard" might be implemented electronically. Further possibilities are statistical measures and data mining for the purpose of performance measurement.

Knowledge Portal. The access tier of the proposed knowledge network architecture is realized as a web-browser-based knowledge portal (IDC, 1999), in order to realize a "single point of access" on the different knowledge objects and systems. Ideally, such a knowledge portal should be configurable and adaptable to the needs of knowledge networks as well as the needs of their members.

Aspects of Technical Integration. The suggested architecture model might be realized as a typical 3-tier-architecture (without the network and integration tier). Underneath the access tier, the server tier and the data tier, the network and integration tier represent the background for this architecture. Today, open and standardized i-net-technologies (i.e. internet/intranet-technologies) are the predominantly used technologies to realize enterprise-wide or worldwide accessible applications. Global connectivity is crucial, since future corporations will have to share knowledge not only within the organization, but also with different alliances, universities, the public, certain individuals, and even competitors located in different places around the world (Högberg and Edvinson, 1998).

An intranet as the existing ICT infrastructure in a company may be used to build the suggested technical architecture. XML (Extensible Markup Language) will play an important role in integrating the knowledge base and the different tiers of the architecture. In the future, new types of mobile terminals and appliances may also be integrated. CORBA (Common Object Request Broker Architecture) and Microsoft's DCOM (Distributed Component Object Model) are "middleware" technologies to realize (distributed) applications within a knowledge network architecture.

Knowledge Network Architecture Scenarios. In the following we describe three typical scenarios of what tool-based knowledge networking might look like. We consider that different knowledge networks require different kinds of tool support.

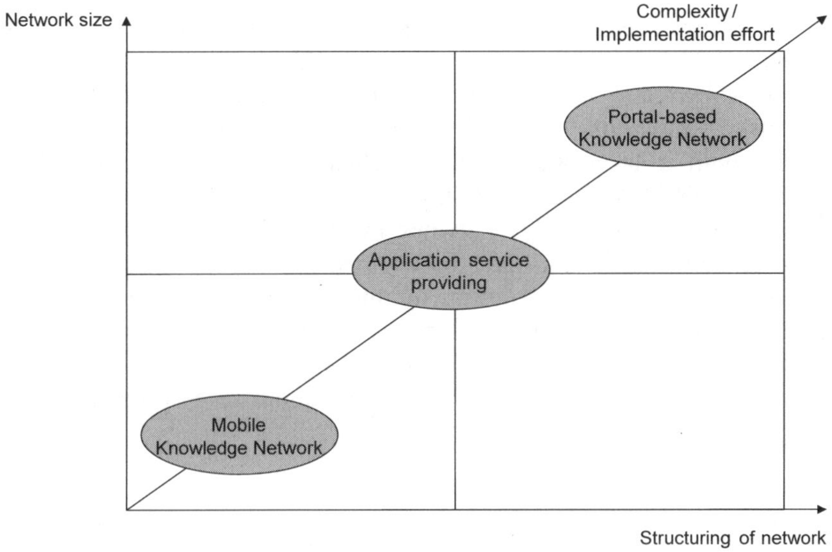

Fig. 15. Overview - knowledge network architecture scenarios

For example, a sophisticated ICT architecture (e.g. a personalized knowledge portal) is not in every case the perfect solution, since for many knowledge networks the implementation effort and the effort to maintain it will most likely be too high. The complexity resulting from particular ICT tool use should therefore never be underestimated. Often, an important success factor for knowledge networks is that the adequate tool infrastructure can be implemented quickly and that implementation and maintenance is not too resource-intensive and time-consuming.

The figure above classifies the three scenarios we have chosen by means of the knowledge network architecture portfolio.

Scenario 1: Portal-based Knowledge Network. A portal-based knowledge network may also be called the "highly-integrated solution". An example of this scenario is the KNOWNET approach which is described at http://www.know-net.org (The Know-Net Consortium, 2000); (for similar architecture models also see Lehner, 2000).

Typically, such a solution is realized on the basis of a comprehensive, often enterprise-wide architecture (reference) model with various layers. The layers are interlinked with each other. A central component is the knowledge server, which includes a knowledge base. The server can be accessed via a web-browser-based portal. Through this "single point of access" users can access their personalized workspaces (Mentzas and Apostolou, 1998).

This kind of solution is usually realized as an enterprise-wide, scaleable knowledge management platform, as several software vendors, e.g. Microsoft, IBM/Lotus, Opentext and others, offer it.

In the knowledge network architecture portfolio, we positioned the portal-based knowledge network scenario as a solution for knowledge networks with a large size, and a well-defined structure. The implementation effort, therefore, is also high.

The underlying knowledge network in this scenario might be a resystematizing network. It also may be an institutionalized learning network which uses a portal-based solution for the purpose of learning (for a detailed description of the different knowledge network reference types see the according chapter).

The following table provides an overview about some pros and cons of this scenario:

Table 5. Pros and cons of the portal-based knowledge network scenario

Pros	Cons
High level of integration with enterprise ICT infrastructure and business processes Advanced functionalities can be implemented (e.g. workflow, intelligent search) Personalization, support of different roles	High effort for planning, implementation and maintenance required Complexity, users need adequate technical skills Inappropriate for task forces, short-terms alliances where a fast and flexible set-up is crucial

Scenario 2: ASP-based Knowledge Network. For many knowledge networks, a portal-based solution, as illustrated in the previous paragraph, might be too large, as too much effort for implementation and maintenance is required. In such a case, application service providing (ASP) might be the right choice. Trends, benefits, and risks associated with ASP have been described in a working paper within the CC (Raimann et al., 2000).

An example of an application which can be rented via ASP, is Lotus Quickplace. An ASP for Lotus Quickplace is Interliant AppsOnline [http://www.appsonline.com].

Lotus Quickplace offers basic groupware functionality such as asynchronous discussion databases, chat, calendaring, library for content management, e-mail integration, task management, as well as administration features (Lotus Development Corporation, 2000); (Wireless Knowledge, 2000). The i-net-based application is accessible worldwide via a web-browser. A main advantage of Lotus Quickplace is that it can be set up very quickly (in minutes), and that users do not need advanced ICT skills. In combination with ASP, effort for administration and customization is reduced to a minimum.

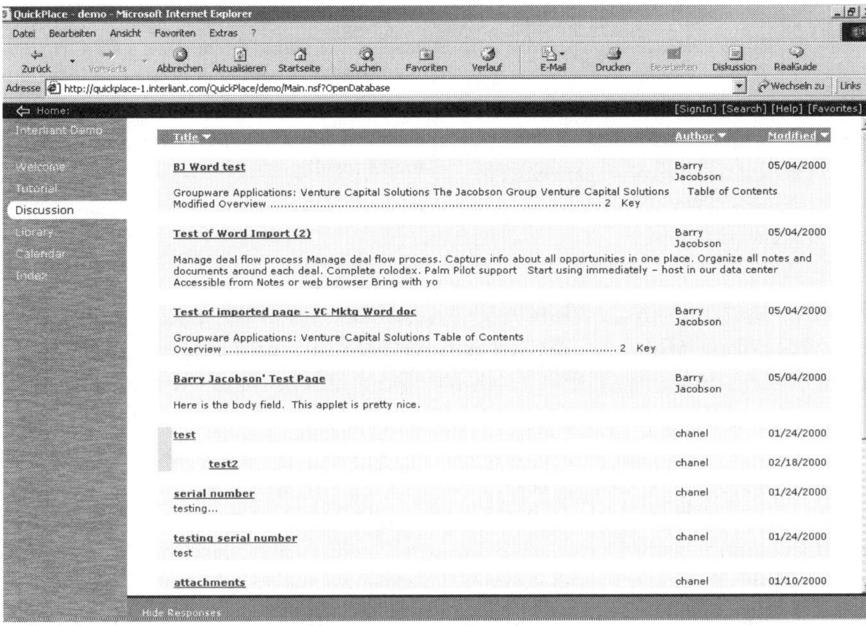

Fig. 16. Example ASP scenario: Lotus Quickplace

Definition

Application Service Providing

An application service provider (ASP) is defined as a company that provides the use of an application – from basic e-mail to enterprise applications – usually via a network or the internet, resp., based on ongoing usage fees. The ASP may host the applications on the customer's site, but most ASPs house the applications at data centers where the ASP is responsible for maintaining the applications and all the associated hardware, software, and network services, to link the applications to the customer base (GartnerGroup, 1999a, 1999c).

With ASP, knowledge networks with a medium degree of complexity may be supported adequately, whereas knowledge networks with a high degree of complexity and high integration requirements should go for another solution. In this case, the implementation effort is rather low, since the ASP carries out the implementation effort. The following table provides an overview about some pros and cons of the ASP scenario:

Table 6. Pros and cons of the ASP knowledge network scenario

Pros	Cons
Very fast setup Simplified implementation and maintenance No workload for enterprise personnel in terms of maintenance Transparent cost	ASP model is not yet approved Low degree of integration with existing infrastructure; "islands of knowledge" might result

Scenario 3: Ubiquitous Knowledge Network. Since there is a major trend towards mobile technologies we believe mobile knowledge networking to be an interesting alternative to think about in the near future. The basic equipment of the members of a mobile knowledge network is comprised of so-called "smart appliances", such as mobile phones, personal digital assistants (PDA), or digital photo cameras. With this equipment, members can be supported in mobile working areas. For example, one might think of individuals as "knowledge scouts" who are visiting congresses, universities, fairs and other events, other companies, customers, etc in order to locate and capture knowledge. Another possibility might be a knowledge network of "creativity agents" who may travel extensively and visit inspiring places, thereby developing new ideas (e.g. for marketing, product development, etc) (Wireless Knowledge, 2000).

Thinking about a mobile knowledge network scenario, one has to be aware that mobile and wireless technologies are changing very rapidly at the moment. Therefore, completely new and advanced devices and applications will be available in the near future. In particular, broadband standards and technologies like UMTS (Universal Mobile Telecommunications System), will provide mobile video, multimedia devices and services. These new forms of connectivity and convergence of telecommunications, multimedia and i-net-technologies, will allow to perform knowledge work processes at any place, at any time. In our opinion this will have a tremendous impact on the capability for knowledge networking (see also Skyrme, 1999).

In our knowledge network architecture scenario, we positioned the mobile knowledge network scenario as a solution for knowledge networks of small size and a low degree of structure. Complexity and implementation effort are rather low, in case standard devices and applications are used and only a loose connection with a central knowledge server is required. Of course, more complex scenarios (e.g. wireless data replication between all network members) and mobile knowledge networks of a larger size are possible.

The following table gives an overview about pros and cons of the mobile knowledge network scenario:

Table 7. Pros and cons of the ubiquitous knowledge network scenario

Pros	Cons
High mobility of knowledge network	Currently costs intensive
Enables new forms of working together	At present restrictions of bandwidth
Providing knowledge services dependent to actual position	Coordination of knowledge network might be difficult

4.3.4 Blueprints of Knowledge Network Reference Types

As stated earlier, the generic knowledge processes locating/capturing, sharing/transferring, creating, and applying can be regarded as the nuclei of every interaction and communication process. Following Nonaka (Nonaka, 1991), these processes can be conceptualized as dynamic transformation-processes between explicit and tacit knowledge.

Socialization comprises the exchange of tacit knowledge between individuals in order to convey personal knowledge and experience. Joint experiences result in new, shared implicit knowledge, such as common values or technical skills. Externalization describes the conversion of implicit knowledge into explicit knowledge. Since implicit knowledge is difficult to express, the conversion process is often supported by the use of metaphors, analogies, as well as visualization aids. The transformation of explicit knowledge into more complex and more systematized explicit knowledge represents the stage combination. This systematization and refinement increases the practical value of existing knowledge, increases its transferability, and makes new knowledge available on an organization-wide basis. Internalization comprises the conversion of organization-wide, explicit knowledge into the implicit knowledge of the individual. Referring to Nonaka we therefore conceptualized four knowledge network reference types, each addressing one of the described dynamic knowledge transformation-processes. These knowledge network reference types can be used to identify "ideal" forms and arrangements in order to contribute to specific business goals. In order to describe the different knowledge network reference types, we use specific knowledge network characteristics. These characteristics have been selected based on their suitability to distinguish the knowledge network reference types from one another. The following figure gives an overview of the relevant characteristics:

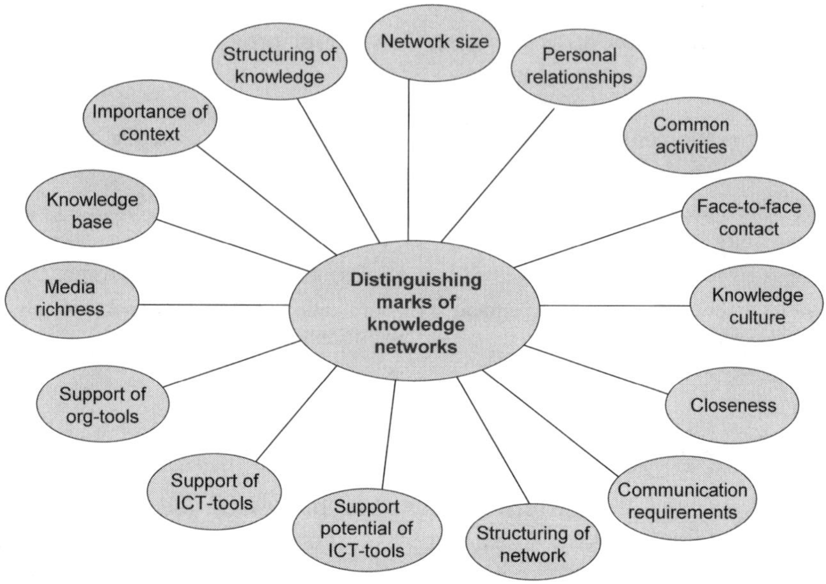

Fig. 17. Knowledge network reference types – classification criteria

What is of great importance is that these characteristics can be influenced by the application of appropriate tools. In doing so, they affect the facilitating conditions for the underlying knowledge processes and therefore can help to achieve a high-performing knowledge network. We now describe the four knowledge network reference types in more detail.

4.3.5 Knowledge Network Reference Type Experiencing Network

Overview

Knowledge network reference type experiencing network mainly pursues the knowledge process of transforming implicit knowledge from one knowledge body to implicit knowledge of another knowledge body. It primarily supports the members to exchange their knowledge, best practices, and solutions through common experiences. In business, this knowledge network reference type has the objective to enable people to interact with other members within the company. In this knowledge network, social knowledge and impressions from inside and outside the company are collected and distributed; for example, directly with customers or through interaction with internal/external experts. On an individual level, people sharing their experiences with suppliers, customers, and with competitors; for example, accumulate implicit knowledge regarding sales. An experiencing network ideally can be described as follows in figure 18.

The degree of these characteristics can be derived from the underlying knowledge process of transforming implicit knowledge into implicit knowledge and the ensuing requirements. Personal relationships are of great importance for this network reference type, since they are most efficient for the transfer of implicit or tacit knowledge (Hansen et al., 1999). Narrow personal relationships are needed on the one hand to create a climate of trust which is necessary for sharing knowledge. On the other hand they are needed fo the actual exchange of implicit knowledge which in this network type takes place more directly through personal interaction.

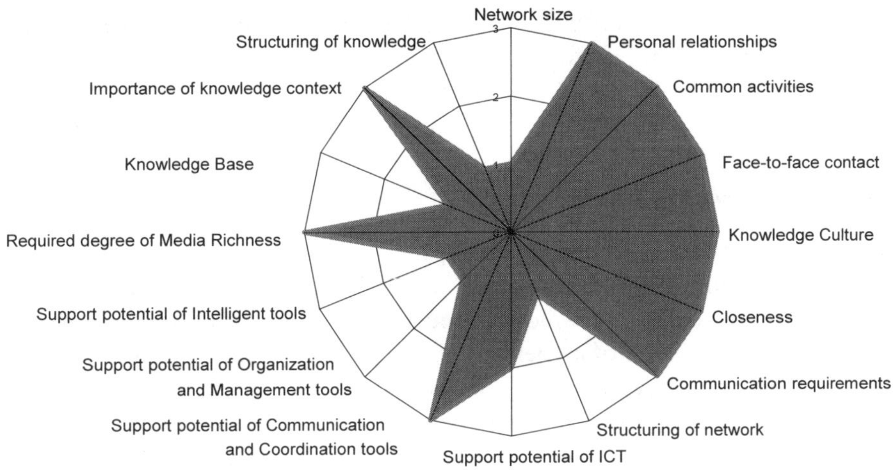

Fig. 18. Characteristics experiencing network

As a consequence of narrow relationships the network size, which is another important network characteristic, has to be rather small. Other characteristics, such as common activities, face-to-face contact, knowledge culture, closeness, knowledge context, communication requirements, degree of media richness, and support potential of communication and coordination tools are very important and highly-distinctive for an experiencing network since these characteristics may support the sharing of tacit knowledge between individuals.

Facilitating Conditions Experiencing Network

In order to achieve a high knowledge network performance, appropriate facilitating conditions inside and outside the network have to be in place. In case of configuring the facilitating conditions for the network reference type experiencing network, the knowledge operational task of transforming implicit knowledge into implicit knowledge has to be considered. According to Nonaka, the exchange of implicit or tacit knowledge takes place "through joint activities – such as spending time together and living in the same environment" (Nonaka et al., 1998). Therefore, the direct interaction of individuals within personal relationships is crucial for the sharing of tacit knowledge. As our research has shown, shared experiences and activities, stimulated by meetings between individuals, as well as the typical values of a "high-care knowledge culture" (e.g. shared trust basis, empathy, and openness) are also of great importance. Other major facilitating conditions are communication aspects. Ideally, there must be a high degree of face-to-face contact, an intensive communication between the network members, which includes long-term interaction and a low degree of lingual and cultural differences. Geographical and social closeness are also required in order to enable sharing experiences as well as context-bound knowledge.

Tools Experiencing Network

With regard to facilitating conditions, the use of tools must be aligned to the needs of this network reference type. The appropriate organizational and ICT tools must be employed and designed in order to support the specific characteristics of experiencing networks. In practice, the process of acquiring knowledge is largely supported through direct interaction with suppliers, customers, and so forth. Another key task is directly disseminating implicit knowledge and sharing personal knowledge (ideas, etc).

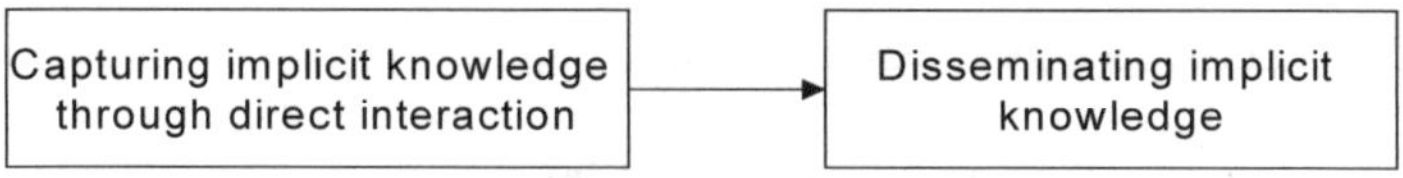

Fig. 19. Knowledge operational task experiencing network

Tools can generally be used in order to support or influence knowledge work processes as well as network building processes. Furthermore, the characteristics of a knowledge network and the structural and cultural facilitating conditions in- and outside the knowledge network, are both influenced by tools. Since intensive communication between the network members is crucial, communication tools are the most important tool class.

Regarding organizational tools, knowledge forums, knowledge workshops, meeting and moderation tools, conversation and negotiation techniques, active listening, and also language tools (dialogue, story telling, metaphors, controlled vocabulary, organizational thesaurus) might be used in order to support communication. Also, many ICT tools can be rather helpful. Virtual communities demonstrate that establishing personal relationships, trust, and sharing experiences and implicit knowledge are to some degree also possible. Therefore, ICT communication tools (especially synchronous technologies and tools with a high degree of media richness) are mostly relevant for this network type. Table 8 gives an overview of relevant organizational and ICT tools to support the knowledge reference type experiencing network.

Table 8. Organizational tools for experiencing networks

Organizational tools
Communication and coordination tools: Knowledge forums, knowledge workshops Coffee corners/talk rooms Meeting and moderation tools, conversation and negotiation techniques, Active listening Language tools (dialog, story telling, common language, metaphors, organizational thesaurus) Organization and management tools: Management tools - conflict management tools - presentation techniques - HMR tools (e.g. job rotation, job enrichment, mentoring/coaching, training and education) - knowledge vision/goals Organizational structure tools - group work - roles and responsibilities (e.g. knowledge activists, community/network roles) Organizational culture tools - change agent - corporate culture change programs - organizational development tools

Profile **Example: Seven Eleven Japan**

Since the customer is often only implicitly aware of these needs, meaning that the needs are only subconsciously present, and that they are difficult to articulate, Seven Eleven attempts to use knowledge networks to promote an experience-exchange that brings forth new knowledge.

In terms of efficiency, Seven Eleven Japan (Nonaka et al., 1998) is widely regarded as one of the globally dominating retail companies. In Japan, the company enjoys the highest return on investment in the retail sector. One of the decisive factors for this is its ability to capitalize on market knowledge. Seven Eleven Japan is organized as a franchising system with 7'000 outlets. These Seven Eleven outlets sell over 3'000 different products, with foodstuffs making up about 77%. Seventy percent (70%) of these products are switched each year. Seven Eleven, being the franchiser, sells knowledge to the outlets, which they use as the basis of their sales policy. In order to be able to offer this service, Seven Eleven has developed a comprehensive knowledge management concept. One of the greatest central elements is the knowledge regarding the needs of the customers and the implementation into new products and services. For this purpose, direct customer contact is sought at the various locations, and this implicit customer knowledge is then shared between the employees of the different Seven Eleven outlets. This knowledge, in turn, is shared at regular meetings with the store consultant of Seven Eleven. These consultants then exchange their experiences in weekly consultant meetings at headquarters. Seven Eleven can attribute its high effectiveness of this procedure to transforming, often only implicitly available customer knowledge. Despite the relatively high effort – exchanging implicit knowledge through personal experience-exchange rather than through information systems – the company's efforts have proven to be worthwhile considering its profitability and its innovation ability (70% product exchange per year) (Seufert et al., 1999).

4.3.6 Knowledge Network Reference Type Materializing Network

Overview

The knowledge network reference type materializing network comprises the knowledge process of transforming implicit knowledge into explicit knowledge. It primarily serves to motivate and stimulate people possessing implicit knowledge to externalize their experiences and thoughts. In this type of knowledge network, individuals having a particular knowledge must be identified and motivated to make this knowledge accessible to others in an explicit form, e.g. in corporate knowledge bases.

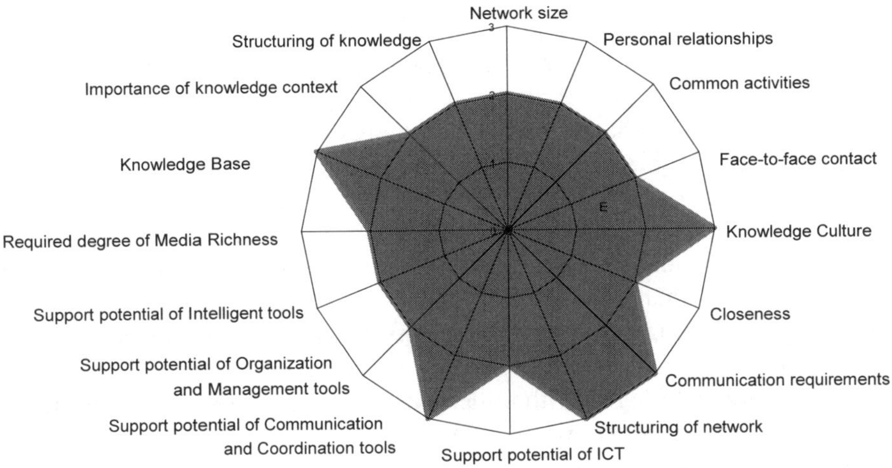

Fig. 20. Characteristics materializing network

An appropriate knowledge culture that provides values such as care, trust, openness, etc, is extremely important in this network type. Without such values, network members will not be willing and able to make their tacit knowledge explicit. Communication requirements for materializing networks are high, since tacit knowledge must be articulated and then translated into readily understandable forms. Consequently, the support potentials for communication and coordination tools are rather high. Since the knowledge that has been made explicit within materializing networks will quite often be stored using a knowledge base, the usage of a knowledge base is very significant. This network reference type should be well-structured, since the process of translating knowledge into an understandable form can be subdivided into different roles (i.e. knowledge authors, reviewers, etc). Personal relationships, face-to-face-contact, geographical and social closeness are important to establish trust. "Common activities" are not as important here as they are in experiencing networks, since the knowledge has not to be embodied by the network members. The required degree of media richness is medium. Quite often, text-based media are sufficient and even more efficient to store and transfer the knowledge. The knowledge itself should be structured to some extent to make its transfer easier. It also should not be absolutely bound to a specific context, since otherwise difficulties in transferring it may result.

Facilitating Conditions Materializing Network

Dialogue and discussion are key for this network reference type. Also, the selection of employees with an appropriate mix of specific knowledge and skills is crucial. The major facilitating conditions for this knowledge network reference type are trust within the network, a high degree of communication, and shared values and interests among the network members. This can be obtained, for example, through communication rules or through the composition of project teams, usage of appropriate tools such as creativity and visualization, and so forth. When designing the facilitating conditions for this network reference type, one must keep in mind two tasks that need to be supported: the articulating of implicit knowledge and its translation into a form that is easy to understand. The task of articulating knowledge is very dialogue-intensive and therefore, opportunities for dialogue with colleagues, suppliers, customers, etc, must exist. Translating the knowledge into an understandable format is less communication-intensive, but requires other facilitating conditions such as clear-cut network roles, sufficient time to structure the knowledge and to put it into a knowledge base, etc.

Tools Materializing Network

Organizational and ICT tools in materializing networks primarily have to support the process of transforming implicit knowledge into explicit knowledge. This process can be subdivided into two parts:

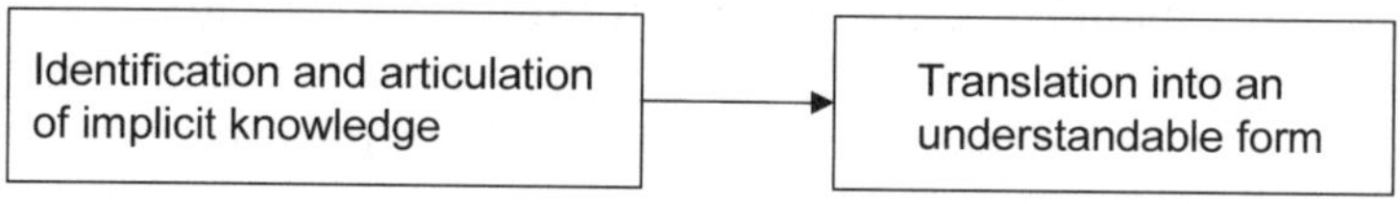

Fig. 21. Knowledge operational task materializing network

First, implicit knowledge has to be identified and then articulated. The process of articulating knowledge is communication-intensive. Therefore, the whole class of organizational as well as ICT communication tools is crucial. Second, the articulated knowledge has to be translated into an appropriate form.

In order to manage the process of bringing the knowledge into a well-structured and understandable format, organization and management tools such as knowledge maps, clear-cut roles and responsibilities, should exist.

Since this process can be intentionally well structured, the utilization of workflow management tools could be effecttive. Intelligent tools, such as skill mining tools to identify experts for certain content areas, may also be incorporated. Table 9 gives an overview of relevant organizational and ICT tools to support the knowledge reference type materializing network.

Table 9. Organizational and ICT tools for materializing networks

Organizational tools	ICT tools
Communication and coordination tools: Knowledge forums, knowledge workshops Coffee corners/talk rooms Meeting and moderation tools, conversation and negotiation techniques Active listening Language tools (dialog, story telling, common language, metaphors, controlled vocabulary, organizational thesaurus and dictionary) Organization and management tools: Management tools - knowledge maps visualization tools - knowledge vision/goals Organizational structure tools - roles and responsibilities (e.g. knowledge authors, reviewers, content manager) - visualization tools - knowledge vision/goals Organizational culture tools - change agent - corporate culture change programs - organizational development tools	Communication and coordination tools: Messaging/e-mail Workflow management Group decision support systems Real/non-real-time conferencing systems Community tools, CSCW-suites Organization and management tools: Visualization tools Creativity tools Intelligent tools: Skill mining Categorization/clustering (e.g. semantic networks, knowledge ontologies) Integration and database tools: Knowledge management suites Data warehousing

Profile **Example: Sharp**

The continued search for creativity and originality has lead Sharp to structure its R&D according to a hypertext model. Part of this organizational model are so called "Urgent Project Teams" that are responsible for strategic development projects.

Sharp (Nonaka and Takeuchi, 1995) was founded by the inventor and craftsman Tokuji Hayakawa in 1912 as a small metals company. Hayakawa was rather ingenious and he motivated his employees to act creatively with statements such as: "Do not imitate, do something that others want to imitate." Since its founding days, Sharp has become known to continually bring forth new products – ranging from a belt buckle that self-adjusts and the Sharp pencil of the early years to the liquid crystal televisions and electronic notebooks of today. Each division can submit urgent projects of this kind which are evaluated by the general technology conference (participants are the president, the heads of competency areas, and the lab managers). Projects which are received positively, are given a maximum project time of 18 months during which they have nearly unlimited access to the resources of the entire company, helping to ensure high-quality developments within short time spans. In order to speedily access core knowledge present in the different divisions, cross-functional teams are usually formed. This could, in certain cases, result in divisions losing their star employees for the duration of the project. The urgent project teams work together with a special corporate design group, facilitating the knowledge exchange between specialists of different disciplines. These designer groups aid the externalization of implicit knowledge, for example, through visualizing concepts in the form of imagery. This, in turn, serves the urgent project teams as input for the development of first prototypes which finally can be used to materialize abstract concepts and, for example, as a basis for discussions in meetings (Seufert et al., 1999).

4.3.7 Knowledge Network Reference Type Systematizing Network

Overview

The knowledge network reference type systematizing network mainly deals with transforming explicit knowledge into explicit knowledge. In this type of knowledge network, existing explicit knowledge is being systemized and refined in organizational handbooks, yellow pages, newsletters, and training materials, in order to reuse it more efficiently. A systematizing network has characteristics as shown in figure 22.

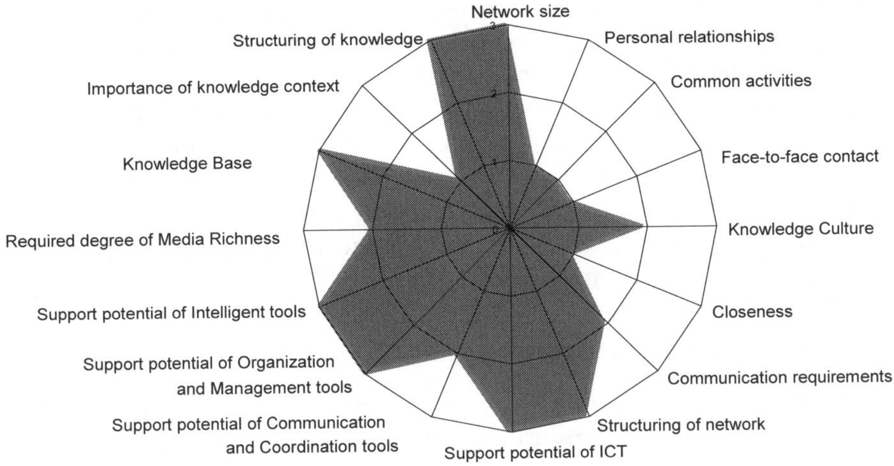

Fig. 22. Characteristics systematizing network

To structure and systematize explicit knowledge, all ICT tool classes can be employed to a high degree. A characteristic of the knowledge itself is that the knowledge can be well structured (structuring knowledge is a main goal of this network reference type). Other characteristics such as personal relationships, common activities, face-to-face contact, as well as geographical and social closeness, are less important since knowledge is not tightly coupled to personal relationships. Due to these characteristics and possibilities of ICT communication tools, the network size and geographical dispersal of it can be rather large. A high-care knowledge culture which provides values such as trust, openness, etc is not as important as it is for the other networks types.

Facilitating Conditions Systematizing Network

When establishing the facilitating conditions, the knowledge process of transforming explicit knowledge into explicit knowledge defines the requirements that must be met. A basic condition is a knowledge culture that ensures that no information hiding takes place or that hiding of explicit knowledge is at least minimized. Further, explicit knowledge should be accessible throughout the company without any restrictions. The knowledge culture and related values must be very "ICT-friendly", since the widespread usage of ICT tools is crucial for this network type. Also, a high degree of consciousness about the possibilities and limitations of ICT tools to transform explicit knowledge is required. This includes reflection on systematizing and structuring of knowledge, including measures to design the related knowledge work processes (capturing/locating, sharing/transferring, creating knowledge) and to adequately integrate them. As our research has shown, other major facilitating conditions for this network reference type are clear-cut roles and a high degree of formalization. Clear-cut roles help to manage the different processes of systematizing knowledge. Roles such as the "knowledge gatherer", who scouts external knowledge, or the "knowledge analyst", who interprets client needs, etc, may be established. The high degree of structure and formalization also helps to manage its size, which can be quite large.

Tools Systematizing Network

To support a systematizing network, a large range of tools should be utilized. This is particularly true for ICT tools. In practice, systematizing knowledge relies on three processes. First, capturing and integrating new explicit knowledge is essential. This may involve collecting externalized knowledge from inside or outside the company and then combining such knowledge. Second, the dissemination of explicit knowledge is based on the process of directly transferring this form of knowledge, for example, through meetings, presentations or ICT tools. Third, editing or processing explicit knowledge will make it more usable.

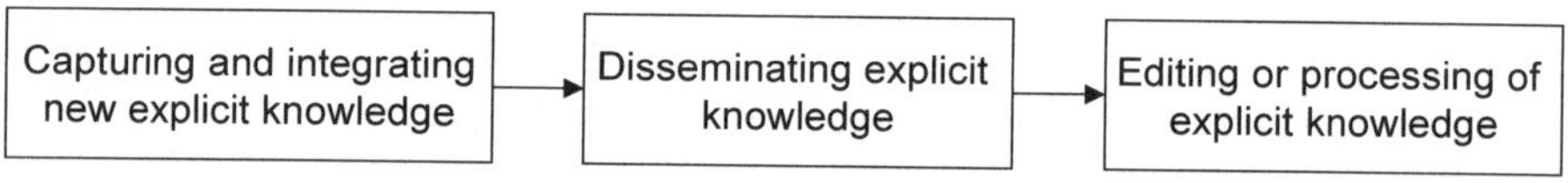

Fig. 23. Knowledge operational task systematizing network

The use of intelligent tools, in particular "intelligent agents", which are able to act autonomously to a certain degree, might lead to a broader understanding of knowledge networks, in which software systems do not only play a role as tools, but rather as autonomous actors beside human representatives (Schmid and Lindemann, 1998). The following table gives an overview of relevant organizational and ICT tools for systematizing networks.

Table 10. Organizational and ICT tools for systematizing networks

Organizational tools	**ICT tools**
Communication and coordination tools: Knowledge forums, knowledge workshops Meeting and moderation tools Language tools (common language, metaphors, controlled vocabulary, organizational thesaurus and dictionary) Organization and management tools: Management tools - visualization tools (e.g. knowledge maps) - rewards and incentives - knowledge vision/goals Organizational structure tools - roles and responsibilities (e.g. knowledge gatherer, knowledge analyst, knowledge author, knowledge reviewer, content manager) - knowledge units Organizational culture tools - corporate culture change programs - organizational development tools - change agent	Communication and coordination tools: Document management/archiving Workflow management Messaging/e-mail Calendaring/scheduling Real-time conferencing systems (A/V conferencing, chat, whiteboard, application sharing) Non-real-time conferencing systems Group document handling Community tools, CSCW-suites, Collaborative filtering Organizational and management tools: Decision support systems Management-/executive support systems Visualization tools Creativity tools Intelligent tools: Intelligent agents Data/text mining Categorization/clustering tools Problem solving tools (neural networks, case-based-reasoning systems) Integration and database tools: Knowledge management suites Enterprise portals Data warehousing

Profile **Example: Accenture**

With over 70.000 employees, 137 locations in 46 countries, and revenues of more than $ 10 billion in 2000, Accenture is recognized as the world's largest and most successful management consulting firm. Because of the "one firm" concept ("act as one firm and speak with one voice"), actions that supported the access and distribution of uniform standards and procedures gained central importance early on. As part of this concept, large parts of the knowledge were stored in the company's knowledge management system Knowledge Xchange. Basic statistical information was stored in databases called jobs, engagements, and projects. A list of all Accenture professionals and their skills could be found in the skills, people, and assignments database. Further specific knowledge bases included core methodologies, industry specific knowledge (visions, major business processes, best practices), discussion databases on various topics, and repositories of or pointers to external information of various types, including technology research and customized news alerts on business topics. This should shorten the learning curve for other employees.

Knowledge capital is our most valuable asset and it drives our organization. It's what we sell, and what we must continue to protect and perfect. Our people should diligently find new ways to share and reuse information and deploy it around the world.

Next to the identification of relevant knowledge, a combination of media and didactical capabilities was particularly important; so as to prepare knowledge in a way that best facilitates learning for others. For this purpose, a team with various experts was assembled. Experienced consultants took part as knowledge managers, identifying relevant knowledge. Furthermore the firm's communities of practice play a central role in Accenture's knowledge management. They are more and more shifting from knowledge sharing, i.e., receiving knowledge from innovative engagements in the field and putting it into a repository for global distribution, to knowledge creation. For instance, they proactively identify leading engagements in a particular core area. Then representatives from each engagement are brought together to figure out the underlying issues and guidelines. As a result the knowledge presented in Knowledge Xchange is synthesized, enriched, and validated. In some areas where the new service offerings are needed, Accenture periodically invests several man-months or even years to re-invent a service offering. The firm pulls together community of practice leaders, diagnoses its own approaches and those of its competitors, and creates a leading-edge approach to delivering the service.

4.3.8 Knowledge Network Reference Type Learning Network

Overview

The knowledge network reference type learning network – comprises mainly the knowledge process of transforming explicit knowledge ("know what") into implicit knowledge ("know how"). It supports the learning, embodiment, and application of existing explicit knowledge. As a result, new implicit knowledge is created. A learning network can be described by the characteristics shown in figure 24.

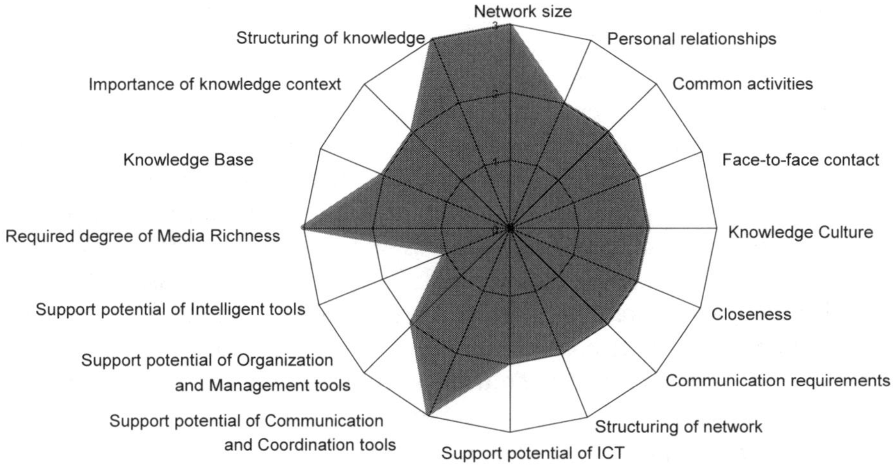

Fig. 24. Characteristics learning network

Most characteristics seem to be of medium distinction within this knowledge network reference type, as depicted in figure 24. An explanation is that this knowledge network reference type has to deal with explicit knowledge and related knowledge processes, as well as with implicit knowledge. First, explicit knowledge has to be identified and understood in its context. Second, there is a process of embodying the explicit knowledge by using simulations, learning-by-doing processes, and so forth. Actually, from a dynamic point of view, the characteristics might vary considerably, since at different stages of transforming explicit knowledge into implicit knowledge, different characteristics are becoming more important. For example, personal relationships, face-to-face-contacts, geographical and social closeness, communication requirements, and common activities are, to a certain degree, not as relevant in the stage of identifying and understanding knowledge. Thereby, one might think about the possibilities of local, personal, individualized, and self-directed learning, etc. However, these characteristics are becoming more important in the stage of embodying the knowledge in action and practice through trainings, mentoring, etc (Haythornthwaite, 1999). Another reason for various characteristics of learning networks is that there are several forms of learning networks with different designs and approaches. Frequently, phases of

ICT-supported learning have to alternate with more traditional forms of learning such as teamwork, training sessions, discussions, etc. Still there are many possibilities to utilize ICT tools (e.g. simulation systems, learning platforms).

Different media also may compensate personal relationships that relay on physical proximity to a certain degree. The knowledge itself in learning networks is not tightly bound to context, since it exists in an explicit form. The transmission of context-bound knowledge might be improved through additional use of context information tools with a high degree of media richness and accompanying practical exercises and tutorials. Also, knowledge in learning networks should be well structured (e.g. in learning modules) to improve learning processes within this knowledge network reference type. The knowledge network itself does not necessarily need a high degree of structure. The process of providing a learning network with explicit knowledge (i.e. content delivery) can thereby be well structured, whereas embodying knowledge must also consider individual preferences.

Facilitating Conditions Learning Network

Central to this type of network is experimenting and experiencing with new knowledge, as well as continuing the application and practice of already obtained knowledge. Learning by doing, experimentation, the trial and error process, experiencing and learning on the job, informal communications, and the simulation of existing problems, are typical processes. Therefore, in order to support these processes, the structural and cultural conditions should enable practice-oriented and continuous learning, exercise and practice of new knowledge, learning from experience, and so forth. The knowledge culture in learning networks should provide values such as tolerance of failures, enjoying experiments, etc. Giving enough time for learning and reflection, as well as helping one another, are also important values within such a "learning culture". Further action-oriented processes to apply knowledge should be supported.

Tools Learning Network

Tools in learning networks primarily need to support the transformation of explicit knowledge into implicit knowledge. Therefore, two (sub-)processes must be supported.

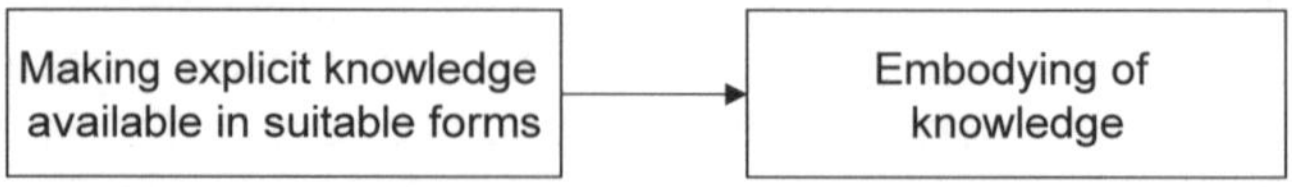

Fig. 25. Knowledge operational task learning network

First, explicit knowledge must be made available in a suitable form (e.g. well-structured, easy to read and understand). A discipline that is specialized in dealing with structuring knowledge for effective learning is for instance instructional design (Seufert and Seufert, 1999). Second, the explicit knowledge has to be embodied through action and practice.

Table 11. Organizational and ICT tools for learning networks

Organizational tools	ICT tools
Communication and coordination tools: Knowledge forums, knowledge workshops Meeting and moderation tools Language tools (common language, metaphors, controlled vocabulary, organizational thesaurus and dictionary) Organization and management tools: Management tools - visualization tools (e.g. presentation techniques, knowledge maps) - scenario learning, planning tools, simulation - HMR tools (e.g. mentoring, coaching, training and education) - learning tools (e.g. learning lessons, learning journeys) - feedback, rewards, and incentives - knowledge vision/goals Organizational structure tools - roles and responsibilities - group work Organizational culture tools - corporate culture change programs - organizational development tools	Communication and coordination tools: Messaging/e-mail Real-time conferencing systems (audio/video conferencing, chat, whiteboard, application sharing) Non-real-time conferencing systems Learning technologies and learning systems for training, such as CBT, WBT Community tools, CSCW-suites Organizational and management tools: Personal Information Management scheduling/calendaring Integration and database tools: Knowledge management suites Enterprise portals

Meetings and moderation tools, visualization tools (e.g. different types of knowledge maps) as well as corresponding roles, support the process of making explicit knowledge available in an adequate form. Within ICT there is a large range of tools to provide access to explicit knowledge for the purpose of learning (Seufert et al., 2001); for example, visualization tools, audio- and video streaming, and community tools. The second process – the embodying of explicit knowledge, whereby communication plays an important role – may also be supported by organizational and ICT tools. Organizational tools consist of various communication tools and organization and management tools (i.e. coaching, mentoring, simulation, scenario learning, and group work). ICT tools that support this process cover the entire tool class of synchronous and asynchronous communication tools, for instance, simulation or modeling tools. Table 11 above provides an overview of organizational and ICT tools to support learning networks.

Profile **Example: Buckman**

The 1996 founding of the Bulab learning center represents an important evolutionary milestone for Buckman in its quest to increasingly abandon its traditional and isolated training units and to search for new approaches.

Buckman Laboratories (Bulab) was founded in 1945 as a specialty chemicals corporation. The fundamental business competence was its unique ability to provide solutions for controlling the growth of microorganisms. Today, Buckman's 1'300 employees generate annual revenue of about 300 Mio. US dollars, serving customers in over 100 countries by providing help in the use and application of advanced technology in the area of specialty chemicals. Since the intense customer orientation requires individual solutions, an average of 86% of Buckman's employees work at client sites. As a response to the extensive innovation dynamics in the area of specialty chemicals, which cause a constant creation and exchange of new knowledge, the Bulab Learning Center was founded. The Bulab learning center is a virtual online-net of learning that makes globally coordinated training and global, multilingual knowledge standards available to the company's employees. Buckman Lab sees this center as a learning and knowledge management tool which is offered to its employees in their usual work environment. The Learning Center makes training and learning available, giving each employee the responsibility and freedom to design his or her own personal and career development. Self-governed learning hereby provides the employees with the opportunity to call upon "learning units on demand" when and where ever they are needed, prompting a continuous performance increase in practice.

Working together in a virtual learning environment allows employees to improve their communication and teamwork abilities, which can only be taught with great difficulty when using traditional teaching methods, but which is essential for a globally active company, as Buckman essentially is. To feed this competitive advantage, Buckman has transferred the responsibility for personal development to its employees (Seufert et al., 1999).

Measurement

4.4 A Knowledge Network Scorecard and Health Check

4.4.1 Introduction

Many say that, what gets measured gets done, but there are many things within organizations that get done without getting measured. It would thus be more appropriate to say: What gets measured gets explicitly managed.

Knowledge management is one of the greatest challenges business leaders face today and will do so in the future (Forbes, 1999; Stewart, 1991, 1994, 1995a, 1995b). Although intangible assets may represent a competitive advantage, organizations do not necessarily understand their nature and value (Collins, 1996). Most managers do not know the value of their own intellectual capital (IC). Often they do not know if they have the people, resources, or business processes in place to make a success of a new strategy. They therefore hardly understand the know-how, management potential or creativity they can access.

Consequently, delivering a positive economic value added must be an act of creativity that emerges from something that is intangible, almost as if it was an artistic concept. The source of this creative energy is IC, i.e. knowledge assets are at least as important as tangible assets. Unfortunately, very few organizations regard intellectual capital as fundamental to their ability to create value. Even fewer organizations establish linkages between intellectual capital and strategy in order to develop and implement cutting-edge processes for measuring and managing intellectual capital. If they are present, they are rarely recognized in internal performance reporting, and even more seldom in external reporting.

Although financial accounting measures and reports on value realization are rife, at present there is no accepted method for reporting on the creation of value. It is undisputed; however, that such a measurement tool should be focused on providing the board of directors and senior management with insights regarding value creation. Such a tool should also be based on indicators, not transactions, and focus on revealing direction and vectors, not absolute quantities. An additional view is provided if this type of accounting perspective is provided in the organizational analysis.

Survey Insights: Measurement

Our survey (Enkel and Wicki, 2002) showed that the performance of 56% of knowledge networks is not measured. Even though there is a considerable difference between large and small networks - in the sense that the smaller the network, the less the likelihood of the performance being measured - there is a potential to identify appropriate measures within knowledge networks. In general, knowledge activities are measured on a corporate level in most companies dealing successfully with knowledge management. Only 18% of the respondents indicated that they would not measure their knowledge activities if appropriate instruments were available. The measurement that is most frequently used is some type of balanced scorecard (24%). Other important measurements for knowledge management on a company level are the intangible asset monitor (18%), HR accounting (12%) or deferred labor costs (8%). However, measuring the performance of knowledge activities appears to be something that is uniquely adapted by each company doing so. A great number of companies experiencing knowledge management use other measurements (30%).

The context for thinking about measuring IC has to start with the apparent aspects: measurement is a fact of organizational life from which there is no deviation. But this does not mean measurement from an accounting perspective only. This awareness helps us to visualize what we are doing, and how the things we do lead to specific business results. Without measurement, intangibles such as knowledge are very difficult to visualize and almost impossible to manage. For a more detailed discussion on the different approaches to measuring IC see Vassiliadis (2000).

4.4.2 An Integrated Measurement System

As research has shown, many attempts have been made to measure intellectual capital and the impact of knowledge. Some examples are: tobin's q, the management value added, the calculated intangible value, various forms of the balanced scorecard, the intangible assets monitor, deferred labor costs, and human resource accounting. Measures that try to assess the impact of knowledge have to fulfill the following criteria (Vassiliadis et al., 1999):

- Is there a direct link between strategy, knowledge, and measurement?
- Is the aggregation of knowledge possible (is there some form of knowledge currency)?
- Is disaggregation possible (can an elementary level valuation be performed)?
- Is there comparability?
- Are all the business areas of knowledge covered (this should include human, structural and customer elements)?
- Are the data that are required easy to obtain?
- Is a frequent and regular compilation of data possible?

Since no direct measurement of knowledge is possible, we propose the use of a scorecard in order to integrate both financial and non-financial performance measures, while explicitly taking knowledge into account. We furthermore propose that the overall business goals for networks and individuals should be translated in an effort to better fulfill the above criteria. In the light of these criteria, the merits of using this scorecard are:

- Measurements at elementary levels and most individual measures can be aggregated right up to the corporation level; it is possible to measure at the individual, the network, and the company level.
- Benchmarking is possible and a regular compilation of benchmarks can easily be done; thus, one can compare networks across a company as well as across companies.

We saw this confirmed in our survey, since most companies do in fact use some form of scorecard to measure their performance. The proposed knowledge scorecard is based on the balanced scorecard (BSC), introduced by Kaplan and Norton in the early 1990s (Kaplan and Norton, 1992).

One of the core ideas in early writings on measurements was to tie the measures in the BSC to an organization's strategy. More recent writings on the BSC stress its development from an improved performance measurement system to a strategic management system. We have adopted this latter view. In addition to linking measures to vision and strategy, measures should be linked to one another, following a series of cause-and-effect relationships. Moreover, a strategic management system involves the use of the BSC for goal setting, compensation, resource allocation, planning and budgeting, and strategic feedback and learning. The BSC has not as yet attracted significant criticism.

A traditional scorecard, however, does not measure knowledge directly. This drawback will be overcome with the IC measurement perspective of the knowledge scorecard. Another limitation of a traditional knowledge scorecard is that aggregation regarding a "common currency" of measures is not possible, but neither is this the primary goal of a scorecard.

The knowledge scorecard aims to not only measure different areas of knowledge impact, such as customers and internal processes, but also different levels of impact, such as the company, the network, and the individual. This is possible, because the knowledge scorecard consists of different perspectives and levels. As such it not only measures the performance of knowledge networks, it looks at the impact of a knowledge network on the achievement of the business goals, risk reduction, efficiency, and innovation, as well as integrating other perspectives. The knowledge scorecard follows a multi-dimensional approach. It retains financial management as a crucial summary of managerial and business performance, but additionally highlights a more general and integrated set of measurements that link current customers, internal processes, and employee and system performance to long-term financial success.

In the accounting literature (e.g. Aboody and Baruch, 1998; Barth et al., 1998a; Barth and Clinch, 1998; Barth et al., 1998b; Baruch and Zarowin, 1998; Birkett, 1995; Bryan, 1997; Deng and Baruch, 1997, 1998; 1998; Leadbeater, 1998), it has been stated that the problem to solve is not how to include IC in financial statements, but rather how to account for the creation of value. The only way to do so is to separately account for financial impact on the one hand, and accumulation of intellectual capital on the other. This is the aim of our scorecard model. Based on performance indicators (using Webster's Third International Dictionary definition of performance "as the achievement of a desired result"), we have developed a measurement model that places these measures within a coherent framework. The knowledge scorecard covers the need to quantitatively measure the performance of knowledge networks according to indicators, which would constitute an external measurement. Still, there are some elements, such as the internal effectiveness of the network, which cannot be measured in such a way. This calls for additional internal measurements, which are qualitative in nature. For this reason, we have also developed a measurement system, which includes – in addition to the scorecard – measuring instruments that can account for the internal effectiveness of the network. We therefore evaluated factors that are essential for successfully building and maintaining a network and integrated them into a double-layered internal measurement system. These additional internal measurements include a “health check” as well as providing the “symptoms of an ailing network”, if applicable.

The latter two internal measurements are analogous to preventative action taken in regard to the human body. Periodically, even when one is feeling well, one visits the doctor for check-ups to ensure that everything is functioning properly. This is the periodic health check to determine if the network is functioning well within the company. The health check takes place:

- directly after building up the network, in order to see whether everything is doing fine and functioning adequately,
- periodically, to see if everything is still functioning according to the specified objectives. In this way, it has a prophylactic function.

It is also imperative to have an alarm system to warn when something is not working properly. These are illness symptoms, so-called “symptoms of an ailing network”. The symptoms of an ailing network and the health check are two independent measurements that help to determine the performance of a network.

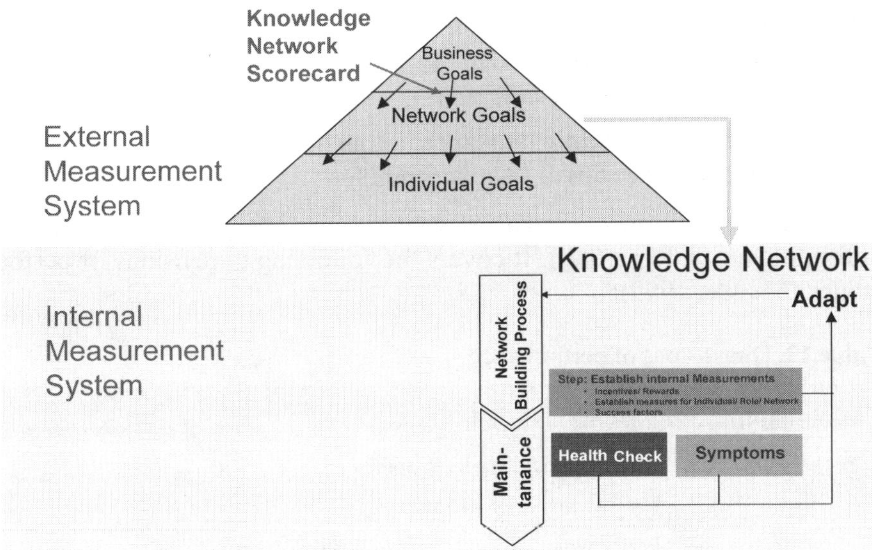

Fig. 26. Integrated measurement system

The symptoms of an ailing network help to categorize failures, analogous to a doctor’s examination, in order to determine the corresponding causes and effects and find the appropriate remedial method.

In order to counteract symptoms of an ailing network, the company has to adapt to the changing circumstances. Both qualitative measurement methods include adaptation possibilities. If the results indicate that it is not worth changing or adapting the network, another option is to let it die.

The figure above provides an overview of the integrated network measurement system.

Key Issue: Measuring the Performance of a Knowledge Network

From our perspective the balanced scorecard (BSC) is a performance measurement tool which, compared to other measurement systems, best fulfills the requirements of an integrated measurement system. It provides executives with a comprehensive framework that translates a company's vision and strategy into a coherent set of performance measures, organized into four perspectives: financial, customer, internal business processes and learning and growth. These four categories help to provide managers with answers to the following basic questions:

- How do customers see us (customer perspective)?
- What must we excel at (internal perspective)?
- Are we able to continuously improve and create value (innovation and learning perspective)?
- How do we perform with respect to our shareholders' perspective (financial perspective) (Kaplan and Norton, 1992; Letza, 1996)?

Like other performance measurement systems, the BSC also follows a multi-dimensional approach. It covers the following dimensions of performance (Merkle, 1999):

Table 12. Dimensions of performance

Dimension	Characteristics
Results	Past-oriented; "lag indicators" E.g. market share and sales
Processes	Performance drivers; "lead indicators" Internal process perspective E.g. time, quality, and price
Resources	Learning and growth perspective Performance drivers; "lead indicators" E.g. intellectual capital (IC), information and communication technology (ICT), and incentive systems

Kaplan and Norton emphasize that the BSC highlights a more general and integrated set of measurements that link the current customer, the internal process, as well as employee and system performance to long-term financial success. In other words, the BSC expands financial accounting to incorporate the valuation of a company's intangible and intellectual assets, such as high-quality products and services, motivated and skilled employees, responsive and predictable internal processes, and satisfied and loyal customers (Kaplan and Norton, 1996). The fact that the BSC integrates different kinds of performance measures, namely quantitative and qualitative measures, lead and lag indicators etc, into various perspectives, is regarded as a main advantage of the BSC by many authors (Ghalayini and Noble, 1996).

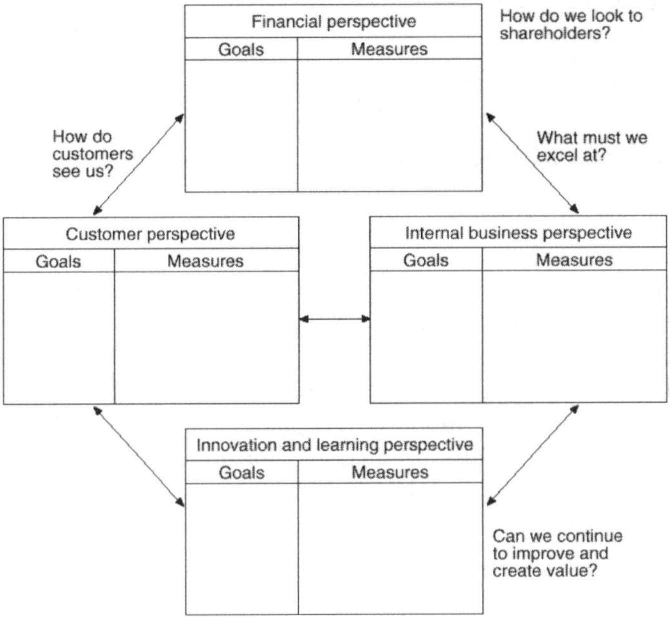

Fig. 27. The balanced scorecard (Kaplan and Norton, 1992)

Fundamental to the BSC is the hypothesis regarding the chain of cause and effect that leads to strategic success. This cause-and-effect relationship is crucial to understanding the metrics that the balanced scorecard prescribes. As outlined in figure 28, there are four stages in this chain of cause and effect (Arveson, 1999).

As the figure shows, learning and growth are key in respect of strategic success and form the foundation for future success. Learning and growth are fostered by knowledge management activities and initiatives. A learning and growing organization is one in which knowledge management activities are applied and expanded in order to leverage the innovation and creativity of everyone within the organization (Arveson, 1999).

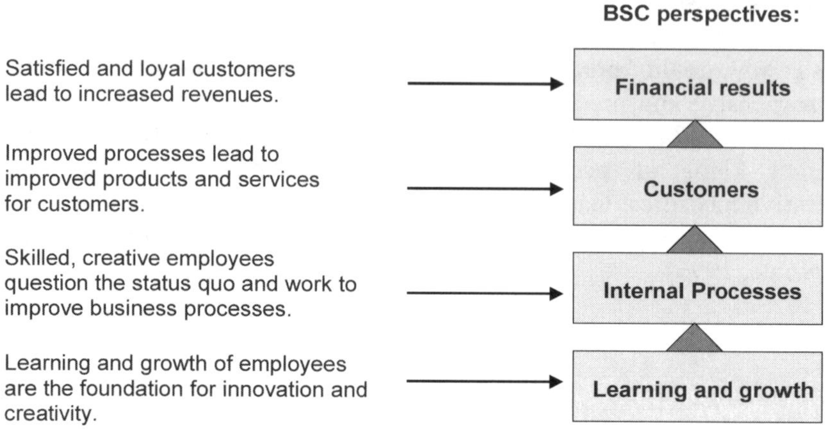

Fig. 28. The balanced scorecard and knowledge management

For a successful measurement system one should follow defined steps. First, it is important to develop a greater awareness and understanding of the role of knowledge and the nature of intellectual capital. Second, the creation of a common language that is more widely diffused within the company is necessary, e.g., the use of terms such as "human capital". In addition, it is essential to identify suitable and appropriate indicators and to develop a measurement model that places these indicators within a coherent framework. Finally, one should introduce measurement systems which include the associated management processes to guide and reward managers. Objective and impartial consultants and surveys could be used to carry out key aspects of the measurement process.

The Knowledge Network Scorecard

The knowledge network scorecard is based on the generic form of the balanced scorecard (BSC). For a detailed discussion of the BSC, please see our working paper series (Köhne et al., 2000; Raimann et al., 2000; Vassiliadis, 1999).

Fundamental to the scorecard is the concept that cause-and-effect chains lead to strategic success. These cause-and-effect relationships are essential to understanding the metrics that the balanced scorecard describes.

The effectiveness of resource usages is judged in terms of the value generated in both, product or service markets (for customers), and capital markets (for shareholders), while satisfying the requirements of other key organizational stakeholders (including suppliers, staff, financiers, and the community at large). Value generation is thus measured from the perspectives of customers or shareholders and from their respective support. Since learning and growth are key to strategic success, and build the foundation for future success, the knowledge scorecard focuses on the learning and growth perspective, which encompasses the development of an internal intellectual capital base.

The construction of a scorecard usually takes place in four steps. First, the requirements of the four key perspectives - learning and growth, internal processes, customer and financial - must be defined. Second, the strategic objectives have to be transformed into quantifiable measures, which help to translate the knowledge management activities for networks. Third, the key persons have to be determined. Fourth, activities have to be set up, which lead to the goals being determined (Bühner and Atitürk, 2000). The strategic orientation of the company will largely determine the goals that need to be focused on. Once the steps have been determined, the knowledge scorecard should pursue the following goals:

- Clarify and translate the vision and strategy.
- Communicate and link strategic objectives and measures.
- Plan, set targets, and align strategic initiatives.
- Enhance strategic feedback and learning.
- Complement financial figures and business goals with IC development.
- In terms of implementation, one has to take action on the following points:
    - breaking down the goals of the company to knowledge goals on the individual level,
    - making them measurable with adapted indicators,
    - developing the knowledge scorecard, including the relevant stakeholders in the development process,
    - developing a pilot of the knowledge scorecard,
    - not allowing counter-productive measures,
    - taking business and fundamental issucs and constraints, which have a direct influence on the company and the network, into consideration.

As these measures are benchmarked either across the organization itself or across related organizations, a "green phase" would signal that performance is above average, whereas a "red phase" would signal a below average performance.

As already stated above, the measurement system consists of measurements done on three levels: company, network, and individual. Regarding the measurement on an individual level, one has to start with the social dynamics involved. In this respect, the individual measurements would perform a monitoring function. Also important is the knowledge flow within the network and how this contributes to the business goals, largely making the knowledge scorecard more of a reporting instrument. Research has shown that the following aspects have to be taken into account when implementing the knowledge scorecard:

On a company level

- The organizational and strategic assessment.
- The portfolio assessment of all the knowledge networks within a company.
- Breaking down business goals.
- Reporting as a function for legitimizing networks.
- The network manager must understand the reporting structure.

On a network level

- The measurement of network performance against goals.
- Risk assessment based on social dynamics.
- Discussing the performance within the network.
- Measures for knowledge flow and for learning.

On an individual level

- Self-assessment for behavioral change.
- Clarifying expectations.
- Usage of the network in a wider context.

On the company level the business goals have to be translated into specific network goals. The company's strategy is thus linked to its knowledge strategy through the knowledge networks. On the network level, the scorecard includes indicators that measure task and process fulfillment with specific reference to the network's task. The scorecard therefore determines if the tasks were executed appropriately. Since the scorecard does not measure whether the network was appropriately built to fulfill its task, this is evaluated by the so-called health check (see below). The network level of the scorecard determines whether the tasks or processes are being fulfilled by the network, and whether they satisfactorily support the business goals. For example, if one of the network's tasks is to improve the innovation process, a measure for this would be the percentage increase in the number of registered patents.

Information on whether a network operates effectively is the outcome of a periodic health check. This health check evaluates the activities and the performance of the network. It enables the direct deduction of concrete actions to be taken in order to achieve the desired result. The results of these measurements are primarily intended for the knowledge manager and the network leader, but should thereafter be communicated to the management. It is crucial that prior to the implementation of a scorecard questions regarding ownership of the results, responsibility for the necessary actions to be taken, and management of the measurement process are clarified.

Figure 29 provides some examples of possible measures according to the defined business goal.

	Company	Network	Individual
Financials 	• Discounted cash-flow • Sales increase • ROE, EVA, ROI	• Profits resulting from operation of KNN • % of R&D invested in basic research in KNN	• Profits resulting from individual involvement • % of input in the innovation process
Customers 	• Customer satisfaction • Retention rate • Customer complaints • % of products < 3 years	• Usage of ICT • % of orders received out of total offers	• Sales per professional • Sales per salesperson • Value added per employee
Internal Processes 	• Time to Market • No. of customer complaints	• % of contracts filed without error • Process cost development	• Employee turnover ratio • Degree of process task fulfilment
Growth 	• Number of patents and cost of patent maintenance • Income per R&D expense • Project life-cycle cost per dollar of sales	• % of new ideas generated to new ideas implemented, • Knowledge Assets	• Number of individual entries to the data base • Qualifications, skills and motivation of employees

Fig. 29. Examples of measures

This figure can also be interpreted as a pyramid, since the overriding business goals are translated to the network and individual level.

When translating these goals into action, one should also take into account the interrelations among these goals and how they affect the individual.

4.4.3 Health Check of the Knowledge Network

In order to measure whether a knowledge network operates effectively, our research identified success factors as being of the utmost importance when building and maintaining high performing knowledge networks. These success factors are clustered and reflected in the health check.
The health check shows how the performance of the network can be monitored from the network perspective, and how certain outcomes can be linked to concrete actions in order to achieve improvements.

This health check is aimed at complementing the knowledge scorecard, especially in terms of linking the outcome with the underlying actions. Therefore the health check is a structured set of questions that either has "yes" or "no" as an answer. These questions correspond to the development steps of high performing knowledge networks, and are derived from the success factors in each of these stages.

An example of a success factor would be good and transparent communication within the network. This success factor is found in the start-up development stage of the network as the element "developing a communication plan" (see the section "storyboard"). Translated into the health check, the question would be: "Is there a transparent communication plan?" Depending on the answer, one would either continue with the next question or move to the corresponding stage in network development (e.g., the start-up section of the building of a network would be relevant).

Once all the criteria on one level have been fulfilled, one would proceed to the next level. Alternatively one could look up the relevant pages and adapt the network. For more details see the section "measure and adapt" of the storyboard.

Symptoms of Failure Leading to Ailing Knowledge Network

In the following we will describe symptoms of failure which can lead to an ailing network. Possible failures will be discussed first. Then these failures will be linked to the characteristics of a network in order to provide insight into which elements or characteristics of the network are critical in an ailing network.

Failure Factors. According to Gierkink and Ruggles (1997), there are several variables that have an impact on the success of a network:

- Missing leadership (or executive sponsorship): This could result in a lack of participation as well as a lack of understanding of the value to be created by a network.

- Missing identity: this might be a symptom of failure, since several networks' experiences show that they had to have monthly or bi-monthly meetings for the participants to really get a sense of who was part of their community and to recognize its value.
- The network coordinator does not undertake any activities to enhance his role as a broker of knowledge.
- Information overload.
- No shared goal.

Hanley (1999) describes factors that promote the primary goals and activities of the networks. These supporting factors strongly emphasize the importance of participation, recognition, and value delivering, and provide important insights into potential network activity failures. According to Hanley, failures and mistakes in a network include the following:

- No recognition of individual achievement.
- No group identity.
- No motivation activities and rewards for participation. No celebration of successes.
- Insufficient delivery of value for individuals, for the company and for the clients or environment.
- Insufficient technological infrastructure.

Foster's paper on "How To Make Communities Work for You" (1999) looks at some important aspects of organization and roles, communities' communication and technology, and also at the questions why communities fail and what their critical success factors are. According to Foster, the following are reasons for the failing of communities:

- Core team members are uncertain about their roles and responsibilities.
- There is insufficient communication within the network, resulting in a feeling of "disconnectedness".
- In general, executives do not regard the community's work and knowledge sharing as important. There is a lack of incentives for community work.
- Required software or hardware for the groupware system cannot be easily accessed, which results in frustration and avoidance of the system.

- There are no proper communication vehicles to match the needs of the network's members, e.g., not having face-to-face meetings, at least in the early stage of a network, in order to build trust and camaraderie among the network members.
- Senior executives do not provide endorsement and continual support.
- There is no readily available and user-friendly technology for communication.
- The network does not have a clear focus or shared purpose, and therefore no real internal reason for existing.
- There are too many objectives, and/or the correct ones are not being focused on.
- There is no learning and experimentation culture.

Further results and insights were gained from our research at Unilever. Derived and interpreted from these, the following issues were also found to contribute to the failure of networks:

- A lack of clarity regarding the role networks and the organization play and the responsibilities they have.
- The roles or responsibilities within the network (regarding work) have not been defined.
- There is no real purpose for and understanding of the network and/or the participants have differing views on its purpose or differ in their understanding of it.
- The intended results or deliverables or targets have not been defined.
- There is a general unwillingness to contribute to the network.
- The principles, procedures, structure and regulation mechanism within the network (regarding functioning) have not been defined.
- The network has not been formalized, but at the same time there are too many formal rules in terms of structure (reporting, etc).
- There is very little time for network members to participate in its activities.
- There is insufficient financial support for the network.
- There is no or insufficient management support or sponsorship.
- The network leader is not really committed to the network, or does not provide sufficient leadership.

- The network leader is too dominant.
- There is no fully dedicated (persistent and considerate) core, coordinating person or group.
- The network members lack commitment to one another or to the network.
- The results or findings of networks are not used or there are no tangible outputs.
- The network participants are not the right people regarding their skills, experiences, and interests.

Additionally, symptoms of failure, such as overspecialization leading to a narrowing of expertise (Miles and Snow, 1986), the lack of a social component in the networks, no real work proposed for or done in the network, the participants' lack of support for one another within the network, or network members not trusting one another, should be taken into account.

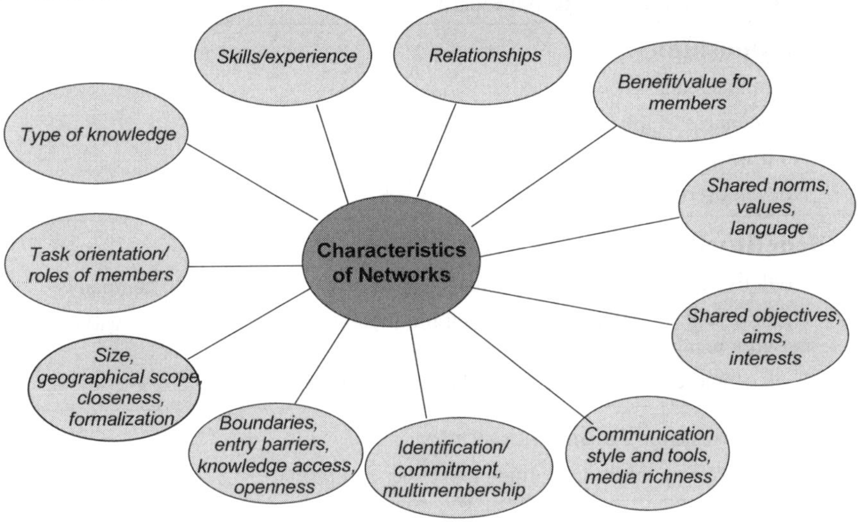

Fig. 30. Characteristics and dimensions of networks

Failure Factors Depending on Network Characteristics. In the following, the failures or mistakes identified in research are linked to the characteristics of networks.

This approach provides insights into how a network's elements or characteristics can predict its failure. As research has revealed, networks have different characteristics and dimensions, which can be clustered as shown in figure 30.

Based on these characteristics or dimensions the failures or mistakes mentioned above can be categorized:

Table 13. Failures and mistakes in networks clustered by characteristics/dimensions of networks

Characteristic or dimension
Task orientation or roles of members:
Uncertainty regarding the network and the organization's roles and responsibilities
No engagement or activities by the network leader or lack of leadership
No definition or uncertainty of roles or responsibilities within the network
No fully dedicated (persistent and considered) core coordinating person or group
A too dominant network leader
Skills/experience:
Not the right people in the network regarding skills, experiences, and interests
Overspecialization – narrowed expertise
Relationship:
Disconnectedness
No openness of the members
No trust in the network
No support of each other within the network
Benefit/value for members:
No delivering of value for individuals, for the network, and for the company
No or a lack of recognition/appraisal/motivation activities for the contributions of network members
Lack of interest in the network by the network members
Shared norms, values, language:
No culture of supporting learning and experimentation
Shared objectives, aims, interests:
A lack of or different purposes/goals for and understanding of the network
Too many objectives and no focus on a selected few
No definition of intended results/deliverables/targets
Communication style and tools, media richness:
Insufficient communication between network members
Information overload
No effective, user-friendly and accessible communication vehicles

Table 13. Failures and mistakes in networks clustered by characteristics/dimensions of networks (continued)

Identification, commitment, multi-membership:
No willingness to do real work in the network
No celebration of successes
No network identity
Lack of commitment to each other/to the network
Boundaries, entry barriers, knowledge access, openness:
No changes for new ideas, or new thinking
Size, geographical closeness, formalization:
No definition of principles, procedures, structure, and regulation mechanism within the network
No formalization, but on the other hand also too many formal rules regarding structure (reporting, etc.)

Additionally, there are also failures or mistakes that can not be directly influenced by the network itself. These failures are strongly related to variables such as the environment of the networks, the embedding of the networks in the organization, as well as the support level of networks. In terms of the overall interrelations of the network with the rest of the company, the focus is on issues that are of overriding and coordinating importance. These failures or mistakes are described in table 14.

Table 14. Failures and mistakes in network that can not be directly influenced

Mission/vision:
Too much pressure on networks; network members and the organization have too little patience
Network members' lack of time to participate
Insufficient financial support of the network:
No endorsement of and continual support from the senior executives; no sponsorship
Results/findings of networks are not used in networks and in the organization/no tangible outputs

The failure "no internal reason for being" is crucial, as it is here where the correlation with the justification for a network solution is mentioned. If there is no evidence as to why the network solution was chosen and to what extent the network contributes to the organization, problems in running and sustaining the network will arise. The network as such will be questioned as long as the network is alive.

It is unlikely that all the mentioned failures or mistakes will occur simultaneously. Moreover, some of them might emerge on certain occasions, and other failures might never appear. Some will be more apparent, and others may barely make an impression. Besides the question of how intensely a failure manifests itself, there is another issue that must be considered. If failures and their influence on networks are to be estimated, their relevance with respect to the network and to its survival must be judged. Therefore, the probability of failures as well as their relevance should be taken into account. The following matrix will help to visualize the importance of failures or mistakes for the network:

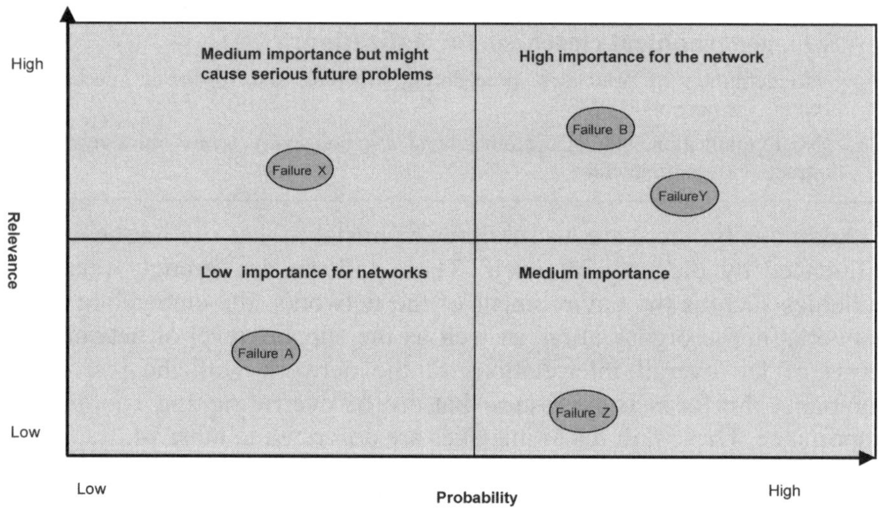

Fig. 31. Probability relevance matrix

5 Storyboard – Setting Up Knowledge Networks

5.1 Introduction

For managers, the importance of knowledge in organizations depends on the practical measures that can be taken in their particular business settings to share, capture, or create it. In this section we elaborate on the building blocks of the concept of knowledge networks in order to manage the knowledge resource itself. In turn, these building blocks provide managers with a framework for setting up knowledge networks. This section, thus, outlines a storyboard for developing knowledge networks as based on our research.

As shown in the following figure, our model consists of five major phases: clarifying the knowledge vision, deciding if the knowledge network is the appropriate option, the selection of the right network mode, the setting up of the selected mode, and the integration of performance measures:

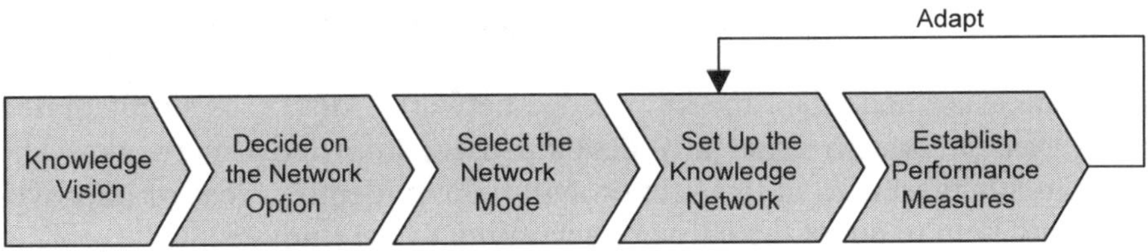

Fig. 32. Overview of the storyboard

The core of the storyboard establishes the roadmap, since it shows how to decide on the network option, and thus identifies a process or task where support of a knowledge activity is particularly needed or where a knowledge gap exists. The clarifying of the knowledge vision in conjunction with the decision on the appropriate tool (which might be the knowledge network) might be considered preparatory work in the sense that they have presumably already been completed in the course of other knowledge activities. It further explains how to select the appropriate mode of knowledge network as well as how to set up the specific network. While setting up the network, performance measurement will become increasingly important. The results of the performance measurement of the knowledge network may necessitate corrective action to the set up process, thus allowing for adaptation within the architecture of the knowledge network.

Our activity handbook starts with the knowledge vision. This vision helps to clarify on what the company's key knowledge is and what it should be in future. Instilling a vision legitimizes the knowledge activities within the company and gives it a sense of direction.

The second part focuses on "decide on the network option." This part comprises clarifying which knowledge is needed and which process should be supported. This leads to an answer to the question whether a knowledge network is an appropriate instrument with which to work.

The third major step includes "selection of the appropriate network mode": research has identified four modes of networks which can be differentiated according to their main knowledge task. This step helps to decide which network mode is appropriate to fulfill the goals set by the company.

The fourth (and largest) part explains how to set up the selected knowledge network: this part comprises the different steps necessary to set up the selected knowledge network mode. Besides dealing with organizing the communication, facilitating relationships within and outside the network, organizing people and meetings and supporting them with appropriate information or organizational tools, this part concludes with the integration of performance measures.

Because performance measurement is important in order to monitor the network action as well as to control its value for the company, the fifth part, "measure and adapt the knowledge network," discusses an integrated measurement system especially developed for knowledge networks. The instruments presented in this section will help to identify areas of improvement and help to adapt the network according to the findings.

To help network managers implementing knowledge networks in their company, the storyboard section of this book concludes with an action plan, which summarizes the major steps in setting up knowledge networks and integrating them in a subsequent project plan.

All the steps are structured in the same way:

- First the topic is briefly introduced.
- Answers are thereafter provided under the heading "Why this is important" and are indicated by a light bulb.
- The "steps to get you there" are indicated by a staircase. They describe the single steps required to implement this network component in your company.

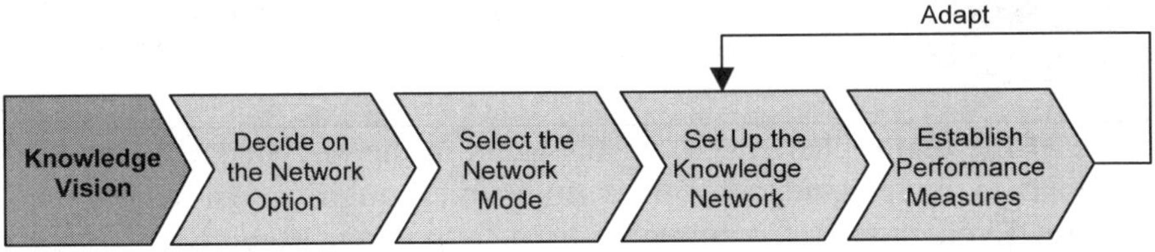

5.2 Clarify the Knowledge Vision

Despite the "cook-book" approach used in outlining the methodology, we must stress that at the beginning of every knowledge management activity there must be a vision of what the company's key knowledge is, and what it will be in future. Instilling a vision legitimizes the knowledge activities – the capture, transfer and creation of knowledge. Nevertheless, these processes cannot be put in place by only managing them. A clearly formulated vision will help the company to more effectively articulate the concepts that support reaching the knowledge goals. Furthermore, the knowledge vision must be consistent with the company's vision. Providing a vision also helps to encourage better utilization of knowledge, and helps to reinforce the importance of the knowledge transfer process itself (von Krogh et al., 2000).

This section will give some insights into creating a vision in order to provide the company with:

- A mental map of the world in which the organizational members live.
- A mental map of the organizational world in which the members ought to live.
- A specification of what knowledge the organizational members need to seek and create.

The knowledge vision is a picture of the knowledge that the company produces and seeks. The purpose of the vision is to generate a certain level of knowledge activity to achieve the desired goals.

Example **A Vision for the Future**

One of the major challenges for managers in the knowledge economy will be to understand what their companies ought to know for the future. Even though the future is hard to predict, executives cannot avoid thinking about what is to come or what might possibly happen. Managers' ignorance can end up being their company's worst enemy. A case in point is the *Facit* typewriter company. At the beginning of the 1980s they, along with other companies, focused on reducing manufacturing costs to stay competitive in a declining industry, rather than focusing on acquiring knowledge of a radically different kind that could have helped them to meet new challenges. Investing in manufacturing assets specific to the typewriter industry tied up their capital and heightened the exit barriers for many companies. While typewriters were gradually replaced by personal computers, typewriter companies continued to cannibalize one another. Holding on to old patterns of justification and existing beliefs, and insisting that typewriters would always have a functional advantage over computers, the company overlooked consumer demand for portability. The current popularity of notebook computers indicates just how detrimental holding on to old beliefs can be.

Why this is important:

- Defining a knowledge vision beforehand is of particular importance because it helps to create the specific roadmap with which to support a knowledge activity.
- Having a clear picture of one's present situation, as well as foresight into future events, reduces the risk of moving in the wrong direction, thereby developing knowledge that may not be important in future.
- Establishing the task of a knowledge network can be done only after, and in conjunction with, the creation of a knowledge vision. This should foster employees' involvement in the company, and will motivate them to view their daily work in a larger context.

Think about it!

- *Commitment to a direction:* The knowledge vision requires a strong commitment from top management. Executives should identify and familiarize themselves with the current

knowledge landscape in which the company is operating, as well as with the future landscape for which they hope.

- *Generativity*: A knowledge vision should spur new thinking, idea generation, and action. It should also spark new organizational imagination and creativity.
- *Specific style:* The knowledge vision should have a specific style (bold, creative, inspiring, and reflecting the "style" of the company).
- *Focus on restructuring the current knowledge system:* The vision should go beyond the experience gained through past successes, e.g., by providing a new interpretation of the strategic history of the company.
- *Focus on restructuring the current task system:* The vision should animate to rethink how work gets done.
- *External communication of values:* A knowledge vision should communicate what kind of knowledge (and hence value) the company will be seeking for all its stakeholders (Enkel and Wicki, 2002).

Steps to get you there:

- Decidc which people you want to involve when developing the vision (top-down, bottom-up, middle up-top down).
- Think of the world in which your organization members live at present: What kinds of disciplines are covered? What technologies are used? What kind of expertise do we have?
- Think of the world in which your organizational members ought to live: Is it possible to merge current disciplines, technologies or expertise? Are there potential new disciplines, technologies or expertise?
- Think of the kind of knowledge that is needed by the organizational members to achieve the future world in which you want to live. What kind of knowledge do we have to acquire or create (this is the starting point of the roadmap)?
- Formulate an open-ended vision and communicate it effectively.

Companies that already possess a vision for their knowledge activities should derive further actions to support knowledge creation from this vision. A knowledge vision should inspire the knowledge network to seek out knowledge in certain areas, and to build up a knowledge resource that can be used to meet future business challenges. Our empirical research shows that 82% of the leading knowledge management companies which responded do have a knowledge vision. A vision is therefore key in giving the company a direction and a sense of the future, and represents the company's specific view on knowledge (Enkel and Wicki, 2002).

The vision should serve as a starting point for developing the specific roadmap presented in the next section. The roadmap will help to identify the current and future realms of knowledge as derived from the vision, and will move it to a more operational level.

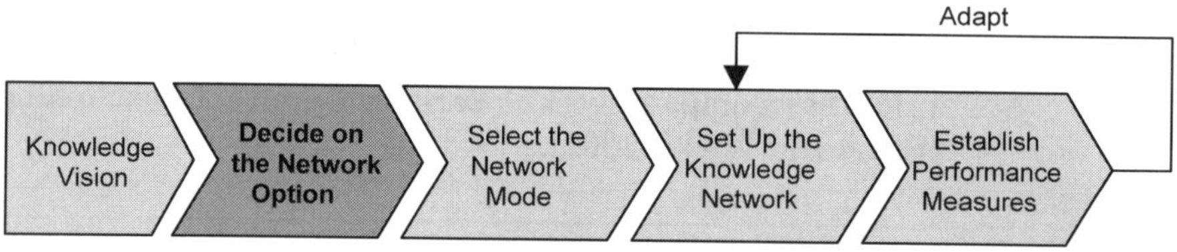

Strategy

5.3 Decide on the Network Option

The purpose of this step is to prepare the set up of the knowledge network by pointing out under which conditions the network is the appropriate strategy to follow.

Specifically, this section includes the following steps:

1. We elaborate on the strategic goals that you want to achieve with your knowledge activity, e.g. risk minimization, efficiency, and innovation.
2. We identify the particular business process or task related to the business goal, so that specific gaps, dissatisfactory knowledge processes, or potential knowledge leverage can be detected, in order to set a clear focus for the analysis.
3. We perform a stakeholder analysis to understand the needs and priorities of the people involved, who themselves have both an influence and stake in the initiative; this also serves as a catalyst by using the

information collected to steer the focus towards the appropriate leverage point.

4. We carry out and describe a deeper analysis of the knowledge which is needed in the selected process or task, which builds the foundation for the next step.
5. The outcome of the deeper analysis brings us to the question whether the choice of the knowledge network is appropriate or not for the particular situation.

5.3.1 Identify Your Knowledge Strategy

Linking knowledge activities to a strategy is crucial. In knowledge management there must be a consistent focus on business value. The alignment of the knowledge actions with the overall goals, i.e. those that are logical strategic goals for all the business units, ensures that all local efforts help to fulfill the company's strategy. Furthermore, the choice of a clear strategic goal lays the foundation for selecting a business process or task and for choosing the appropriate knowledge activities.

But what business objectives should be our focus in managing knowledge? Research has identified the following key business objectives (von Krogh et al., 2001):

Risk optimization: *"We have to discover what we have and record and save it before it is too late!"* e.g., reducing supply chain costs, sharing of best marketing practices, sharing of human resource practices, and leveraging product development costs across subsidiaries.

Efficiency improvement: *"We must make what we have easily accessible to the organization - and find new uses for existing knowledge!"* e.g., dealing with uncertainty in government policy making, competitors' reactions to your strategies, the risk of over-taxing your resources, and dealing with the risk of knowledge becoming outdated. The knowledge activity should also help to achieve innovation goals.

Innovation increase: *"What we have is not sufficient for creating a knowledge-based business: We need to enable the creation of new knowledge,"* e.g., creating new products and service innovation to meet consumer needs and building unique and lasting customer relations.

The selection of a business goal, e.g., risk efficiency and innovation are key in order to focus the new knowledge activities, such as the set up of a knowledge network. The business goal helps to determine the knowledge strategy: achieving the business goal by deliberately planning the knowledge network. By selecting this goal, the choice of the appropriate business process or task for knowledge action becomes clearer as well.

5.3.2 Select and Understand a Process or Task

To follow the identified strategy you have to focus your knowledge activities on the business process or task in which you identified either a knowledge gap or a leverage point to improve knowledge management activities. In order to achieve the strategic goal identified in the previous section, a sample of business processes or tasks becomes relevant.

Why this is important:

- Understanding the processes allows you to focus on the project without losing sight of the big picture.
- The process or task has to follow the strategy.
- You may focus on an innovation process, an efficiency improvement process or a risk optimization process.
- It is also possible to find a gap in your knowledge management that you may want to close, or a knowledge leverage point where you may create a new process or task.
- If you keep in mind where you want to go in the future, the knowledge vision should guide you there.
- Only when you understand when and where people need to act, and therefore have to use knowledge, you can understand what kind of knowledge and what kind of knowledge activity are needed.

Think about it!

- Get out of your area of expertise – your company may be generating revenue through a process/processes that you do not fully understand. If this is the case, you will need to

collaborate with people outside your department or, possibly, even outside your company.

- Follow the money – which products and services are the most profitable? How can you build a knowledge management initiative to make these products even more profitable?
- Existing processes may not be formalized anywhere; the one you pick may be outdated or lacking in expertise, and you will probably not be able to outline it by just sitting at your desk. In this case, convene a series of short meetings with your in-house experts, executives or others who can steer you into the right direction.
- How important are the people and organizations outside your company or department? Try to understand the roles they play in achieving the business objectives. Try to find a gap in your knowledge management.
- Which competitors will you have to confront to achieve your goals? Understanding how to defeat them can be a key objective.

Steps to get you there:

1. Examine your knowledge vision, your long range planning, and the specific business objectives. These three tasks will help you to identify a selection of business processes or tasks.
2. Set your focus on the particular selection, and investigate which of these processes or tasks could be improved by a better handling of knowledge and need to be supported through new or improved knowledge activities.
3. Try to understand these processes while focusing on the knowledge that is needed to implement them.
4. Identify the gap you want to close with your knowledge activities and describe it in detail.
5. Possible gaps can be: a) a lack of a particular skill, expertise, or knowledge; b) a minor identification process of the knowledge available; c) a lack of knowledge distribution and sharing, as well as simply d) ineffective knowledge creation.
6. Pick one business process or particular task that you want to

support with knowledge activities and describe the new process or task your knowledge activities have to fulfill.

5.3.3 Perform a Stakeholder Analysis

The purpose of the stakeholder analysis is to understand the needs, priorities, and ideas for action of those who will influence the success of your knowledge management initiatives. Or to understand the needs, priorities, and ideas for action of those individuals affected by the activities including senior managers, business-unit leaders, functional and staff support groups, key external partners and suppliers, internal clients at various levels, and others.

Why this is important:

- The stakeholder analysis forms the foundation for checking the chosen business process or task you identified in the previous step. Do the stakeholders regard this chosen process as important for the knowledge activity, and do they see the potential that its improvement could provide?

Think about it!

- It is important to use the stakeholders as an additional source of input when identifying the process, gaps or leverage that you want your new knowledge activities to initiate.
- Through the involvement of the always-important stakeholder, you minimize the risk of false action and you help to reinforce the commitment to your new knowledge activities.

Steps to get you there:

1. Identify the main stakeholders related to knowledge management activities, as well as the specific names and positions of people who represent those stakeholder groups.
2. Identify the expectations of stakeholders in respect of the selected business process or task or knowledge leverage points that you consider most important.

3. Document the anticipated and preferred positions of stakeholders: current and future requirements; "ideal" requirements in terms of knowledge, and recommended actions – be sure to carefully think through the preferred position of each stakeholder, and how to approach them during discussions when testing hypotheses about how they can most effectively support your knowledge management efforts.
4. Conduct interviews (formal or informal) with a representative sample of stakeholders from key areas.
5. Ask stakeholders where they see the gap or where knowledge management activities have to start as soon as possible. Show them your vision and the process, gap, or knowledge leverage point where you see a potential to make better use of knowledge.

5.3.4 Understand the Different Types of Knowledge Needed

The identification of the necessary knowledge as well as its sources (such as the people or a group) with which to support the process or task to ultimately achieve the business objective is critical. This step serves as the basis for choosing the appropriate knowledge activity.

Why this is important:

- This stcp helps build a framework for understanding how knowledge is used in your chosen business process or task.
- Once you have identified the business process, task, or leverage point, you are ready to identify the necessary knowledge and the people who provide, use, or even create such knowledge at each point.
- You are striving for an understanding of how content fits into each part of that business process or task, and how to prioritize it.

Think about it!

- The knowledge needed at each point of the business process, task, or closing of a gap should reflect the knowledge vision – it should consider the future needs and direction of the company.

- The knowledge identified at this step should complement the knowledge strategy. An assessment of whether this knowledge enhances the competitive advantage should also be made at each step is the knowledge:
  - valuable?
  - rare?
  - difficult to imitate?
  - without substitutes?
- Obtain a consensus or a general understanding of the knowledge and where it is needed in your selected processes and tasks.
- Make sure that the knowledge identified is in line with the expectations mapped in the stakeholder analysis.
- Ask yourself and others where information is acted on in your chosen business process.
- Do not get hung up on perfection. Most business processes are not always precise, nor are the tasks that have to be supported by the knowledge management activity clear-cut.
- Talk to managers who govern the process. They should have a handle on who is involved and what the issues are in terms of new knowledge needed.
- Do not limit your focus to people in your company. Consider people outside the organization as well.

Steps to get you there:

1. Break down the process or task, or describe the knowledge leverage points you want to use at every stage where people use knowledge, and map this.
2. Get involved and learn how the business process or task works in terms of the expertise used. Or define all the actions or requirements you need to carry out and fulfill with your new knowledge initiative.
3. Start by identifying those events where people need to act most effectively to facilitate the process.
4. After you have identified the people involved at each point in the process or task, you will have to identify the knowledge they need.

5. Interview others to find out what is important.
6. What are the relevant job titles?
7. Ask the identified individuals about inefficiencies or knowledge gaps in the process or task. Many people have a good understanding of where the success or failure lies in such processes.
8. Who is responsible for effective and successful negotiation at each point in the business process or task? Interview the people who govern the process.
9. Talk to the people who are recognized performers in the process. What can they tell you about who is involved?
10. Spend some time assessing the most important pieces of information used at each point in the fulfillment of the process or task.
11. After identifying the knowledge you need, the knowledge you have and the knowledge owners for your chosen process or task, you are able to plan the knowledge activity that is needed to speed up the process or task fulfillment.

5.3.5 Decide on the Network Option

The purpose of this step is to determine whether the network is the most appropriate knowledge management solution in respect of the information you collected and analyzed in the previous steps.

Why this is important:

- In order to support a specific business process, task or knowledge leverage point, you could use different organizational forms or different knowledge activities. For the success of your knowledge initiatives, it's very important not only to identify the appropriate points to act on, but also to choose the appropriate form for your activity.

Think about it!

Ask yourself questions such as:

- What are the consequences of your choice? What are the interests of your stakeholders? How do competitors deal with the network option? What are the industry trends affecting resource allocations within the company? Are there network skills and capabilities within the company?

- Is the company culture qualified to support a new organizational form like knowledge networks? E.g., does this form fit the company bonus or incentive system? How does the network option fit into the overall business strategy? What is the business orientation?
- Consider the resource requirements related to the network option:
  - Which kinds of resource characteristics do we have/do we need?
  - What is the degree of asset specificity?
  - How frequently do transactions take place?
  - Are there complementary resources?
  - How easily can our resource rights be protected?
  - Are we dealing with heterogeneous demand?

Steps to get you there:

1. Take a look at your analysis of the chosen process, task, or knowledge leverage point.
2. Use the collected evidence of the knowledge you already have and the knowledge you need in order to achieve the strategic goal.
3. Combine this with the map of the knowledge owners and the stakeholders' needs.
4. Use this information to help you choose the appropriate knowledge initiative to achieve the defined goals.
5. Identify all potential knowledge activities that are suited to this analysis and think about alternative organizational forms.
6. Perform a SWOT analysis to compare different forms to deal with knowledge.
7. Check whether the existing types of knowledge, the given architecture and culture fit the network approach in order to select the appropriate network and organizational form for your knowledge activities.
8. Clarify management commitment/preferences.
9. Check the resources required for each organizational alternative.
10. Consider the cultural, technical and economic circumstances of each solution to determine what is the most appropriate.

Learning Case

Merlin Netty is a young knowledge manager at a music instrument company, the SoundSource Corporation, which is a leading international company in the production of musical instruments – from pianos and drums to violins. Her target focus for upcoming knowledge management activities is to support innovation in the processes and tasks of SoundSource to better enable the company to achieve its strategic goal.

In order to achieve the innovation target, she analyzes a selection of processes, tasks, and knowledge that could be leveraged. The particular process of getting musicians involved in the innovation process has room for improvement. Even though SoundSource has an internal "idea box", the employees' inputs are rarely considered and carried out. Merlin also realizes that there are two potential knowledge leverage points. First of all, SoundSource produces different instruments in different countries; consequently, the specialists in charge of treating the materials of the different instruments in those countries could communicate, thereby supporting and encouraging the exchange of experiences and the sharing of insights. Second, setting up a knowledge transfer process in conjunction with universities or other research facilities could speed up and bolster the innovation process. After analyzing these issues, she concludes that the deliberate support of the knowledge exchange between the local material specialists might have the largest impact on reaching her strategic knowledge goal.

Before she starts implementing these initiatives, Merlin first analyzes exactly how the material specialists work, which processes they must use to treat and test the material for the instruments, where they work and on which instruments, and what their deliverables are. Then she identifies possible cross-country connections between the specialists. Prior to kicking off these activities, she first consults the various stakeholders in the different development processes of treating the materials of the various instruments. She inquires whether or not they see any significant potential in supporting this process with a knowledge network or if the support of any other process is more crucial. All the stakeholders agree that Merlin's idea of supporting the specialists' developing and testing of differently treated materials for SoundSource's instruments with knowledge activities would help everybody involved. However, they also stress that the activity needs to be focused to obtain the greatest benefit. In this situation, Merlin identifies the knowledge areas and their sources, the apparent gaps, and analyzes whether or not the activity is worth supporting. It is also crucial to mention that these specialists would be mainly dealing with tacit knowledge.

The results of her analysis reveal that this selected process would benefit from some type of knowledge activity. She takes various methods and organizational forms that she has already encountered into account. She could also organize regular conferences or develop an electronic platform on the internet where the specialists could exchange documents or other pieces of codified knowledge. But, due to the fact that these developers would mostly be exchanging tacit knowledge, the option of creating and building up a knowledge network would seem to have the potential for a far superior effect on the knowledge exchange and development.

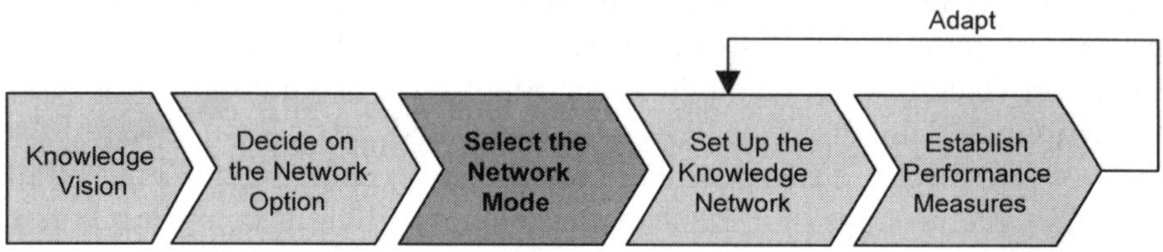

5.4 Select the Appropriate Network Reference Type

Knowledge Network

The last section provided the framework for taking a snapshot of the existing situation in your company. Now you can determine whether building up a new organizational form – a knowledge network – is the appropriate choice for your planned knowledge management activities. This section builds upon this and helps you to select the appropriate network reference type for the task you want to complete and the knowledge you need in your company.

First, a brief description of the different knowledge types will be given in order to clarify the various knowledge network reference types. In addition, a learning case will illustrate the application of those modes in a practical setting. Second, the typical forms of the different knowledge network modes will be introduced together with their particular facilitating conditions (for a detailed view of the reference modes). Third, with the information on the typical characteristics of each, you will be able to select the appropriate network reference type. A matrix will be used to identify the deliverables.

5.4.1 Types of Operational Knowledge Tasks and Types of Knowledge Created

In order to support your process or task with regard to knowledge and the management of knowledge, choosing the appropriate network mode is key to determining the most prevalent type of knowledge in the process. Here the fact that the knowledge could either be explicit or tacit plays an important role, since explicit knowledge is more schematic and easier to transfer systematically than tacit knowledge. In addition, the function of the network mode is determined by its operational knowledge task. In turn, the operational knowledge task has an impact on the appropriate facilitating conditions of the network. For example, if the knowledge network is mainly a network of experts supporting an innovation process by creating a new corporate innovation process description, the key operational knowledge task of the network would be to turn tacit (experts') knowledge into explicit knowledge by codifying it. It is thus made accessible to others. The network mode would be a materializing network.

In the previous section, we identified the following four operational knowledge tasks and the resulting network reference types:

- Experiencing knowledge network: combines tacit knowledge and creates new tacit knowledge.
- Materializing knowledge network: transforms tacit knowledge into explicit knowledge.
- Resystematizing knowledge network: combines explicit knowledge and creates new explicit knowledge.
- Learning knowledge network: transforms explicit knowledge into tacit knowledge.

The result of the transforming and combining processes within the particular network is new knowledge. To better illustrate this, we can identify the contents of the knowledge created by the four network reference types (adapted from the SECI model of Nonaka and Konno, 1998).

In an experiencing knowledge network, sympathized knowledge, such as shared mental models and technical skills, is prevalent. On the other hand, in a materializing network conceptual knowledge is created in the form of analogies or metaphors. In a resystematizing network, systemic knowledge, such as prototypes or new technological components, is created. Finally, a learning network gives rise to operational knowledge, for example, project management, production processes, or policy implementation (see Nonaka and Takeuchi, 1995).

FROM \ TO	tacit knowledge	explicit knowledge
tacit knowledge	*Experiencing Network:* sympathized knowledge	*Materializing Network:* conceptual knowledge
explicit knowledge	*Learning Network:* operational knowledge	*Resystematizing Network:* systemic knowledge

Fig. 33. Content of the knowledge created

Profile **Resystematizing a Knowledge Network**

A team of Andersen Consulting consultants was installing an order management tool of the SAP R/3 information system package for a consumer goods manufacturing client in South Africa. The information system – based on the popular SAP enterprise software – would allow the client to process orders more efficiently. The implementation was scheduled for Monday morning of the following week. On Thursday afternoon, the Andersen team's project manager was worried. Part of the implementation involved an interface with a manufacturing and supply chain planning system, but the team had never tried to put these two systems together before. In order to develop the interface, the team had written the software code in SAP's programming language, but the program ignored the data that came from the interface. The team turned to an Andersen Consulting knowledge network for help to solve the problem. They began their search by posting a question in a discussion database dedicated to SAP issues to see if anyone had experience with the specific problem the team had encountered. After a few minutes a consultant working in Singapore replied to the posting in the database, saying that his team had faced the same problem just three weeks earlier. The consultant provided the solution in his reply. On reading the documents, the project manager identified a piece of software code that he could extract from the document and use to solve part of his problem. Trusting that the knowledge he had obtained was relevant and of high quality, he was confident that he could solve the unforeseen problem he and his team had encountered. By resystematizing the explicit knowledge provided by the network, he achieved systemic knowledge in the sense that he created a new solution for the customer and thus new knowledge.

5.4.2 The Facilitating Conditions Determine the Knowledge Network Reference Type

This section will introduce the different network modes as described by their facilitating conditions. Facilitating conditions are the circumstances in which the knowledge network activities take place. They can enable or hinder the operational knowledge task. We argue that when setting up a network, company-related facilitating conditions are pre-determined and are largely not directly influenceable by the network itself. On the other hand, facilitating conditions within the network can be influenced directly or indirectly.

In the following section you will find a brief overview of the facilitating conditions of our four knowledge network reference types, and to what extent they have to be in place within a particular network reference type. Structural facilitating conditions are, for example, the size of the network and the particular skills present. In contrast, cultural facilitating conditions are represented by trust, values, and the style of communication. Using specific tools, which will be described in the following section "set up the selected network", can influence the facilitating conditions and the creation of a specific reference mode.

The Experiencing Network's Characteristics

When compiling the facilitating conditions of the network reference type experiencing network, an operational knowledge task of transforming tacit knowledge into tacit knowledge is a prerequisite.

The following facilitating conditions characterize the experiencing network:

- Direct interaction between individuals within personal relationships.
- Shared experiences and activities.

- Values associated with a "high-care culture" (e.g. shared trust basis, empathy and openness).
- A high degree of face-to-face contact, intensive communication between the members, including both short- and long-term interaction (e.g., meetings versus one-week workshops).
- A low degree of lingual and cultural differences.
- Geographical and social proximity.

The Materializing Network's Characteristics

An operational knowledge task of transforming tacit knowledge into explicit knowledge implies the use of a materializing network reference type. According to Nonaka and Konno (1998), dialogue and discussion are keys for this knowledge network reference type.

The following facilitating conditions characterize the materializing network:

- An appropriate mix of special knowledge and skills, and interdisciplinary combinations of groups.
- Trust within the network.
- A high degree of communication.
- Shared values and interests between network members.
- Sufficient time to structure the knowledge and put it into a knowledge base.
- Appropriate organizational tools with which to support the materializing of tacit knowledge, i.e. clear-cut roles, and communication rules.

The Resystematizing Network's Characteristics

When configuring the facilitating conditions of the knowledge network reference type resystematizing network, the operational knowledge task of transforming explicit knowledge into explicit knowledge is crucial in order to satisfy the structural and cultural requirements.

The following facilitating conditions characterize the resystematizing network:

- The knowledge culture has to ensure that no information hiding of knowledge occurs, or that the hiding of explicit knowledge is at least minimized.

- Within the company knowledge can easily be accessed, and there are not too many restrictions.
- ICT tools are widely used.
- A high degree of awareness of the possibilities and limitations of ICT tools is necessary. This must consider the resystematizing and structuring of knowledge, including measures to design the related knowledge work processes and to adequately integrate them.
- There should be clear-cut and special roles.
- There should be a high degree of formalization.
- It could be rather large in size.

The Learning Network's Characteristics

The operational knowledge task of transforming tacit knowledge into one's own tacit knowledge is crucial in order to satisfy structural and cultural requirements.

The following facilitating conditions characterize the learning network:

- Central to this type of network is experiencing and experimenting with new knowledge while simultaneously applying and maintaining knowledge already obtained. Therefore, learning by doing, experimentation, trial-and-error processes, on-the-job learning, informal communications, and the simulation of existing problems are typical courses of action.
- Structural and cultural conditions should enable practice-oriented and continuous learning, should exercise and apply new knowledge, learn from experience and so forth.
- Values such as tolerance of failures or experiments and openness should be fostered.
- Sufficient time for individual learning and reflection, as well as for working together is of great importance.
- There should be action-oriented processes to apply knowledge.
- There should be learning within a learning environment.

5.4.3 Identified Deliverables Determine the Appropriate Knowledge Network

A clear focus must be articulated in order to manage a knowledge network properly. This includes agreement on the operative goals. The main operational task of a knowledge network defines the purpose, the work and the outcomes. We therefore use the main operational task to identify the appropriate knowledge network mode.

Why this is important:

- You have a clear focus on dealing with the most valuable resource in your company.
- If the wrong operational goal is set, and an inappropriate network mode is chosen, the performance goals of the network are harder to achieve.
- Setting the proper goals initially will better determine the other parameters of the network.

Think about it!

- The main operational task is embedded in the company strategy and the specific business processes. Consequently, the work of the network has to suit these aspects.
- Trade-offs between the company, network, and individual goals must be considered.
- A particular knowledge network can pursue several operational tasks. However, only one task is especially suited for the network and can lead to higher performance. The network resources and commitment should therefore focus on the main operational task.
- Trade-offs between different tasks should lead to a clear and explicit definition of the main task or to any required adjustments.

Steps to get you there:

1. Identify deliverables:

   The analysis in the last section, and the collected information on the process, task or the identified knowledge leverage point, will now help you to choose the appropriate knowledge activity that can most effectively support the strategic goal. Review the analysis from the last section to make a more educated choice.

2. Identify the knowledge and choose the appropriate knowledge activity:

   In order to identify one's operational knowledge task, consider the following questions that examine two different perspectives:

   a. **Input perspective:** What is the most prevalent type of knowledge with which the network deals (explicit/tacit)? Which type of knowledge has to be leveraged more effectively and efficiently – is it the existing tacit knowledge or the existing explicit knowledge?
   b. **Output perspective:** What type of knowledge does the output of the network entail (explicit/tacit)? Does the new knowledge ultimately have to be in an explicit or tacit form?

   The answers that correspond to (a) and (b) help to identify the main operational knowledge task:

   1. (a) explicit and (b) explicit: resystematizing network
      The main operational task of this knowledge network is to systemize and refine existing company knowledge.
   2. (a) explicit and (b) tacit: learning network
      The main operational task of this knowledge network is to learn, embody, and apply existing explicit knowledge.
   3. (a) tacit and (b) tacit: experiencing network
      The main operational task of this knowledge network is to have the members exchanging their tacit knowledge, best practices, and solutions through interaction and common experience.
   4. (a) tacit and (b) explicit: materializing network
      The main operational task of this knowledge network is to have knowledge "owners" or experts communicating their tacit knowledge in an explicit form through language, and thus capture their knowledge in documents or other forms.

The following table provides an overview to help with the selection of an appropriate network.

Table 15. Matrix with which to select the appropriate network reference type

Knowledge	Experiencing Network	Materializing Network	Resystematizing Network	Learning Network
Tacit to Tacit				
Tacit to Explicit				
Explicit to Explicit				
Tacit to Tacit				

Further Questions that Can Help You Make an Appropriate Choice

- What knowledge will be needed in future to achieve the selected strategic knowledge goal?
- Is it possible to codify your existing tacit knowledge in an explicit form?
- Reconsider the requirements acquired through the selected business process, the task or the knowledge leverage point that you want to support.
- What knowledge content is given (see section 5.4.2)?

Learning Case

After deciding that a knowledge network would be of great benefit to the material specialists, Merlin now has to decide what this knowledge network is actually going to look like. Her analysis of the processes, the specialists' daily work and what part of their knowledge is used shows that even though the specialists are using very clear and structured development processes and research data, much tacit knowledge is present. It is mostly present because these particular processes and data are dependent on the researchers' individual experiences and background, which may cause varying opinions on which testing methods and processes are appropriate. This knowledge is mostly exchanged amongst them through anecdotes and casual conversation.

A young developer who has just joined the company needs to spend much time with his/her coach in order to acquire and improve his/her skills. Once again Merlin reconsiders the future network's deliverables in order to focus on increasing innovation. The operative goal of the network must be to deliver explicit knowledge of the treatment of material and to make the tacit insights and experience of that process explicit. The aim of the network she wants to set up is to capture, share, and create knowledge across the country's material specialists, and further leverage it to other countries - and thus make it explicit. Here, a materializing network is most appropriate.

The main operational task of this knowledge network is to let knowledge "owners" or experts communicate their tacit knowledge in an explicit form; through language by capturing their knowledge in documents or other form of externalization. There will have to be a high degree of communication between those involved, and sufficient time to structure the knowledge and put it into a knowledge base, which, in Merlin's opinion, would be possible. Achieving shared values and the interest of the network members could prove to be more difficult. But, taking SoundSource's culture into account, she believes this will not be a problem. The real work is about to start – she must facilitate the start-up of the knowledge network.

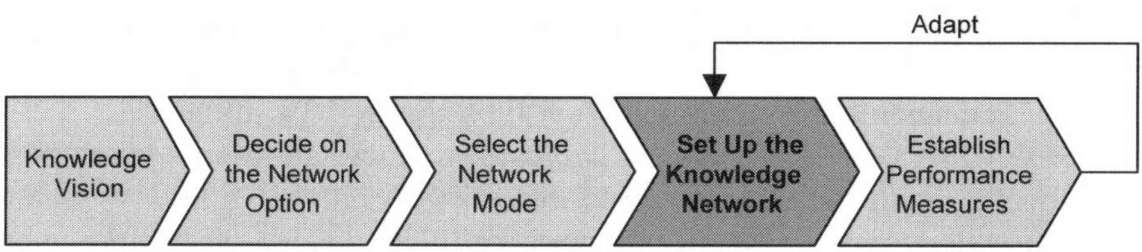

5.5 Set Up the Selected Knowledge Network

Knowledge Network

Having identified the appropriate network to support their processes and tasks, we now show managers how to set up the particular network. A knowledge network integrates the components of the type of knowledge as well as its members and their relationships into a powerful working relationship. Building your knowledge network means putting processes and tools in place in an environment that enables the management of knowledge. This section is about the creation and development of a knowledge network. However, when setting up a high performing knowledge network there should also be an awareness of the interdependencies between the different building blocks of a knowledge network.

The first part of this section shows what is required to launch the knowledge network. First of all it is key to justify the concept and to plan its communication to help attain top management's commitment. After having mapped the specific goals, tasks, and activities of the network, the concrete processes within the network can be organized using a functional network map.

The second part of the section shows that the relationships within the networks must be established in order to get the knowledge network operating. Once the tasks, goals, and activities of a particular network have been defined, the roles and responsibilities within the network need to be established. This helps to illustrate the network on an organizational level, to know where the people are within the organization and what they do. Second, meetings between the appropriate people need to be organized. Third, in order to achieve a fully operating knowledge network, the network members' commitment must be secured; there should be an obligation to contribute to the network that originates from the appeal of being associated with the network. Fourth, there should be a knowledge-enhancing environment to support the people and the processes necessary for completion of the tasks within the network as well as appropriate facilitating conditions being present for each network. Finally, an organization of ICT architecture can provide the network members with an appropriate framework with which to achieve the ideal facilitating conditions by, for example, enhancing the communication flow through the intranet.

The third part of this section is dedicated to facilitating and developing relationships with the outside world. Specifically, it shows how to establish a knowledge management board so that it can keep a watchful eye on the company's strategic direction. It also shows that a broker can potentially provide the knowledge network with the necessary external support, for example, by solving problems among network members in respect of competing tasks by coordination and integration with other functions.

Finally, the last part of this section discusses knowledge network performance measurement. Appropriate internal rewards and incentives must be in place before one creates performance measures for individuals, their roles, and the entire knowledge network level.

5.5.1 Start-up

The aim of this step is to initiate the entire process; that is, to identify the specific area or process within your company which you want to support by a knowledge network.

Justification and Communication Plan

The goal of the justification process and the communication plan is to show that the knowledge network is ready to garner the support and acceptance of top management and sponsors in order to obtain resources such as time, money, and people. Thorough explanations of the justification of the knowledge network, in addition to a well thought-out communication strategy, are key.

Why this is important:

- The need for the knowledge network must be apparent in order to spark people's interests and to motivate them to participate.
- A timely communication of the purpose, the goals, and the on-going successes of the knowledge network can have an impact on the ability of the network to attract members.

Think about it!

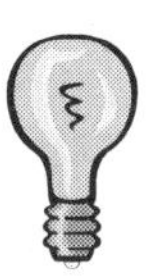

- The justification for network building is directly drawn from and linked to the company's knowledge vision and thus defines the vision of the network itself.
- Think of how you would communicate failures.
- Assigning an individual to be responsible for the communication may be useful.

Steps to get you there:

1. Define the key mission, values and benefits of the knowledge network as based on the knowledge audit.
2. Makes sure that the knowledge vision and values are in line with the company's mission and values.
3. Clarify the network's tasks.
4. Develop a communication strategy for:
   - top management,
   - the people involved in the start-up,
   - the individual/potential members,
   - the entire company.

5. Decide on what you want to communicate to whom and when.
6. Consider the channels of communication.

Facilitate Top Management Commitment and Find Sponsors

The commitment of top management is a critical enabler for a knowledge network. Convincing top management of the importance and merits of a knowledge network is key when seeking out sponsors to provide appropriate resources, as well as when wishing to evoke the personal interests of the managers involved.

Why this is important:

- Top management commitment is crucial to the success of any effort aimed at changing the operational philosophy of the organization. Without management commitment the knowledge network is most likely to dwindle at some point in time.
- When an organization attempts to establish a knowledge network, members are more likely to invest time and effort if the network has the full and credible support of top management.
- Without top management recognition, some members of the knowledge network will not fully commit themselves.
- Top management support is needed when additional resources are demanded.
- The benefits of top management commitment are:
  - quality is given a higher priority than cost cutting, thereby providing adequate resources for the implementation of the knowledge network,
  - there is investment in human and financial resources,
  - it is possible to make the knowledge network a dimension in performance evaluations throughout the organization.

Think about it!

- Resources can eventually be committed elsewhere and other projects can claim top management's attention.
- knowledge network's initiators can obtain commitment through the proven success of prior projects.
- Previous successful knowledge initiatives can support the awareness and importance of the resource "knowledge" and the necessity to deal with the resource.

Steps to get you there:

1. Spend time with key people.
2. Be enthusiastic:
   - create awareness of the importance of knowledge and communicate the vision,
   - be clear about your strategy.
3. Make benchmark studies.
4. Clarify measurements: make mid- and long-range plans in terms of measuring the impact of the knowledge network.
5. Show and explain the resources that are needed.
6. Give top management the opportunity to participate in the knowledge network as resident experts.
7. Clarify top management's means of control and intervention.
8. Communicate the successes, failures, and achievements of the knowledge network from time to time.
9. Show the impact of the knowledge network on performance and thus, on the strategic goals.

Map Your Specific Goals, Tasks and Activities

Having communicated the strategic need and business goal of the knowledge network, as well as the business processes supported by the network, the activities, tasks, and intermediate goals must be assigned.

Why this is important:

- The mapping of the specific goals, tasks, and activities helps to organize the knowledge network.
- The goals determine the competencies and skills needed in the knowledge network.
- This step is key to help establish the measurements of the knowledge network.

Think about it!

- The knowledge activities support the strategic goals and are deduced from the company as well as from the knowledge vision.
- A common understanding of the task and activities is key in order to obtain commitment from future members.

Steps to get you there:

1. Identify the knowledge network's intermediate tasks and goals.
2. Specify the knowledge content needed for the achievement of the goals.
3. Specify what skills and competencies are needed in the knowledge network.
4. Indicate the possible sources of the knowledge, information and data for the activities.
5. Articulate your goals, tasks, and activities and make them visible.

Organize the Specific Processes

The specific processes in the knowledge network, derived from the goals, tasks, and activities identified in the previous section, have to be organized.

Why this is important:

- In terms of capturing and locating, sharing and transferring, and finally creating knowledge within a particular knowledge network, the processes within a knowledge network need to be articulated.

- A full understanding of the specific processes is necessary before they can finally be organized or supported.

Think about it!

- Concentrate on specific knowledge.
- Leverage successful existing processes.
- Look for links between different processes.
- The mapping of the goals, activities, and tasks has to be the starting point of this step.
- Think of your strategy when you organize this process:
  - Is knowledge managed efficiently?
  - Are there any risks related to the process?
  - Is innovation being fostered in this process?

Steps to get you there:

1. Identify the knowledge identification and capturing processes for the fulfillment of your knowledge network's tasks.
2. Identify the knowledge sharing and development processes for the fulfillment of your knowledge network's tasks.
3. Identify the process with which knowledge is developed.
4. Map those processes according to the task and the consequent knowledge content and skills required.
5. Observe knowledge networks directly for a more in-depth description of the processes.

5.5.2 Mapping Processes and Roles

The following figures map the roles and their corresponding knowledge work processes, as well as additional major tasks for each knowledge network reference type. The circle around the map signifies the facilitating conditions that build the network and support the operational knowledge task.

Facilitate the Relationships within the Network

After solidifying and organizing the processes of the knowledge network, relationships within the knowledge network have to be developed. It is particularly important to find people with certain skills who represent different roles within the network, so that the spirit of the knowledge network can be brought to life. In order to ensure full commitment, these knowledge network members must be motivated and supported by appropriate and, most likely, different means.

As a first step in this section, we examine the roles and responsibilities in a knowledge network on a general level and thereafter elaborate on the kind of roles that are generally key within a knowledge network. Further, the different roles specifically defined for a particular network, are identified according to the skills needed, the roles of the participants, and the specific function of the knowledge network leader. Second, potential members are identified and meetings are organized. Third, articulating the benefits and designing clear-cut responsibilities enhances people's commitment. The last two steps in this section show which organizational and ICT tools can help support people in a specific knowledge network.

The enabling and facilitating of the knowledge network are fundamental. These supporting factors of the knowledge network have the same effect as sunshine has on a plant: without them the network will not grow and prosper.

Determine the Roles and Responsibilities

Assigning the roles and responsibilities in the knowledge network creates a minimal structure within the network and provides a starting point from which to achieve a high level of member commitment.

Why this is important:

- Defined roles provide the knowledge network with a certain structure. A knowledge network's structure may, however, be dictated by the task it has to fulfill. The concept of roles comprises the behaviors that a particular function or position within a knowledge network requires. To a significant degree, the existing roles determine the network members' behavior patterns. After determining the roles, clear communication of the responsibilities for certain actions within the knowledge network has to follow.

- In order to make responsibilities within knowledge networks explicit, roles can be deliberately created and be allocated to specific members.
- Knowledge networks run into problems when roles are not initially allocated, or when there is ambiguity involved. Some overlap in roles is, however, useful in that people learn from one another and provide help during a colleague's absence.

Think about it!

- There are different kinds of roles for different responsibilities in the knowledge network. In addition to roles, leadership is required to fulfill and organize the knowledge work processes. These roles are necessary in all modes of knowledge networks.
- There are specific knowledge roles that need to be allocated. They are roles such as *sponsors*, who are managers in top- or middle-management who support the network initiatives, (e.g., assigning resources) and communicate the results and needs of the network to the top management.
- The *knowledge manager* coordinates the knowledge network's work with other knowledge work within the company and builds the bridge to other networks or knowledge activities.
- The most important role for every network is the *network leader*. He/she defines and manages the activities of the network members, sets priorities and is responsible for the relationships with the outside world.
- *Knowledge workers* can be active and passive participants of the network. The active members work on knowledge topics, fulfill and shape processes and foster the architecture, depending on what the specific network task requires. The passive members of the network are participants who are not yet willing and/or able to actively participate; at this moment they only obtain knowledge from the network. However, in the future they can increase their activity in the network and thus transform themselves into active members.

Steps to get you there:

Each role is designed using a specific profile, namely the skills that are required and the actual position this role should hold within the organization. Certain responsibilities stem from each role. To better ensure the commitment of the network members, it is useful to present every potential new network member with the role and its corresponding responsibilities. Therefore, documenting the specifics of each role is helpful (see table below). This could lead to a discussion about the true meaning of a particular role, which in turn should help to establish the network member's commitment.

Sponsor

Profile: top management.

Responsibilities: member of the knowledge management board; building the bridge between the knowledge network and management; communicating the results and the needs of the network to a higher level.

Knowledge manager

Profile: middle management.

Responsibilities: motivator and guide for the knowledge network; bridges the knowledge network with other knowledge activities, projects and networks throughout the entire company; knows external and internal experts who are not members of the network.

Network leader

Profile: acknowledged expert with a high degree of social skills (e.g. promotes care and trust within the network).

Responsibilities: communicator, moderator, motivator, and representative of the network; organizer, coordinator, and integrator of the network activities; supports a high-care network culture.

Members

Profile: interested in the special knowledge topic of the network; may be experts in a specific knowledge topic or have special capabilities needed in the network (e.g. IT-specialist).

Responsibilities: active contributor in the network; fulfills tasks given by the network leader; communicator of the work and the results of the network to the outside world; bridge to other business units, employees, or companies.

For each individual role, list the responsibilities, the related tasks and targets (see table below), and discuss them with each member or potential member. He/she should give his/her commitment to these with his/her signature.

Table 16. Responsibilities, tasks and targets of a specific role

Name: Role:

Responsibilities:	Tasks:	Target:	Date:

Outlining the responsibilities, tasks, and targets offers the additional advantage of knowledge transferability from a departing network member to a new network member.

Experiencing Network: Roles and Skills

Roles of Participants. In experiencing networks, the exchange of tacit knowledge is less structured and often occurs subconsciously. It is therefore more difficult to establish and document many task-specific roles in an effective manner. Since the network members obviously perform certain roles, these roles can be better characterized as team roles with particular corresponding skills. Some of the typical knowledge roles, such as a "knowledge activist," might exist in this mode of network, while here technical skills are not that important, as they are within a resystematizing network. Nevertheless, these skills are required to a certain extent in order to deal adequately with communication technologies. As a member of this type of network, a technical expert or media expert should know which ICT tools are relevant for this network reference type and how to deploy them properly. Therefore, he or she should have some knowledge about and experience with synchronous and asynchronous communication technologies. However, skills related to other technologies, for example, building up a knowledge base, are not as important.

Skills Needed. In experiencing networks, communication skills that enhance and foster communication and discussions are of great importance. Other useful skills are superior negotiation, conversation, and active listening techniques. A thorough analysis of the communication systems currently in place may help to uncover critical gaps and potential areas for improvement. Furthermore, high-quality team working skills are required for this network reference type. Social abilities and "soft skills", such as sensitivity, willingness to cooperate, tolerance, readiness for consensus etc, are key requirements within experiencing networks.

Network Leader. Network leaders in experiencing networks should possess skills to moderate face-to-face meetings between individuals. As a moderator, the team leader has to take on several roles: initiator, motivator, promoter, visionary, coach, mentor, etc. The network leader must also have the skills to deal with the given knowledge culture, the company's underlying values, and the entire process of sharing tacit knowledge. A network leader should therefore know how to establish trust in an experiencing network. He or she should also be aware of social processes happening within work groups and teams, and know how to deal with them, so that he/she is able to motivate people to share their tacit knowledge. Also, given that internal conflicts negatively attribute to performance within this type of network, excellent conflict management skills are required. Overall, the network leader should be highly skilled and experienced in, and considered to be an expert on, interpersonal relationships.

Materializing Network: Roles and Skills

Roles of Participants. Roles within materializing networks may focus on turning unstructured knowledge into structured knowledge. For example, the role of knowledge editor could concentrate on formatting and outlining conversations, correspondence, and emails. Another role is that of a content expert or book owner, who represents the central and main contact for a specific content area. Facilitators in meetings are also important within materializing networks, since they can help evoke certain creativity, and support other network members to express their ideas.

Skills Needed. Network members in materializing networks require proper communication skills in order to articulate themselves and express their tacit knowledge and to communicate successfully with others (e.g., customers and colleagues) in order to capture tacit knowledge. In these tasks reflective processes are of great importance, since they enable network members to apply techniques for evoking creativity from others, and to visualize thoughts and opinions. Members have to know how to effectively use theoretical language through story telling, analogies, and metaphors, in order to create concepts, hypotheses, and models. The ability to deduce certain aspects from specific solutions, and then apply them to create universally valid approaches, is another type of skill required. Turning abstract concepts into usable ideas, and then putting them into actual practice, is also advantageous. Further, at least some network members should possess certain publishing skills in order to present and express knowledge in a way that it is easily understandable to all. Technical skills are also required in order to deploy ICT tools adequately. For example, network members need to know how to add knowledge to a knowledge base (regarding structure, format, meta-information, etc).

Network Leader. A network leader in a materializing network needs specific skills and know-how to manage the process of transforming tacit knowledge into explicit knowledge. He/she should know which type of knowledge can be made explicit, which knowledge is worthy enough to be made explicit, which tools are suitable, and so forth. Additionally, he/she should know the time and effort necessary to make knowledge explicit. It is also crucial that the network leader knows how the knowledge transformation process should be structured and which roles should be established. Motivating network members to externalize their experiences and thoughts and to make contributions to a knowledge base, should also be the responsibility of the network leader. A network leader should also be aware of what will not motivate network members, of how disappointments and failure can be avoided, and how to keep the overall materializing process alive.

Resystematizing Network: Roles and Skills

Roles of Participants. The various tasks inherent in a resystematizing network should be structured and formalized, in order to improve efficiency and reduce complexity. The resulting roles, such as section author, knowledge gatherer, knowledge analyst, or knowledge reviewer, require suitable responsibilities. For example, a knowledge reviewer must possess expertise in the respective knowledge area.

Advanced technical skills are particularly important for network members who have the role of media expert within a resystematizing network. They must not only understand the role that certain ICT tools can play in knowledge networks, but they also need a feeling for and understanding of the needs of the network members. Since the use of ICT requires considerable support activities (e.g., technical support, support for the maintenance of the knowledge base, security, backup, etc), adequate support mechanisms within or outside the knowledge network must be in place.

Skills Needed. To a greater extent than in other network reference type, network members' technical skills are crucial for the success of a resystematizing network. This includes the appropriate selection of hardware and software, which should carefully be chosen and adapted to the individual situation. Also important are practical skills as well as ICT considerations, checklists and guidelines on how to use them.

Further, network members need specific skills to deal with explicit knowledge; in particular, how to manage the process of structuring and "resystematizing" it, and how to improve its quality and relevance. Quite often an online resource or knowledge base will play a central role within a resystematizing network. Creating and maintaining such a knowledge base also requires certain highly specific skills. Challenges that exist and need to be faced are how to identify and pre-filter knowledge, how to contextualize it, and how to enable and stimulate the reuse of knowledge. Additionally, communication skills should not be overlooked in resystematizing networks since, as stressed before, skills to work with ICT communication tools play a central role.

Network Leader. Network leaders in resystematizing networks need skills to "virtually" manage and control a knowledge network. For example, they need to know how virtual discussions and conferences can be carried out and moderated. Typical leadership functions, such as motivating network members, ensuring the usage of ICT and a knowledge base, and ensuring performance and quality, will also often take place virtually in this type of network. These "virtual" leadership tasks in resystematizing networks require appropriate tools (e.g., ICT-based performance measures) and skills as well.

Learning Network: Roles and Skills

Roles of Participants. In learning networks the roles of tutor, coach, and mentor and their corresponding responsibilities and required skills will have an important function, either for the whole network or within smaller groups in this type of knowledge network.

A media expert within a learning network must excel in the area of learning, as well as in the necessary and associated technologies.

Skills Needed. An important prerequisite for members in learning networks is their willingness and ability to learn. Apart from intellectual abilities to acquire and assimilate new knowledge, members of a learning network might need additional skills such as self-management skills, to help manage the, quite often, time-consuming learning processes and then integrate them into their daily work. Skills and techniques to manage information overload (e.g., personal information management), to orientate oneself within the organization, to identify the knowledge relevant for one's self, as well as the individual virtual learning techniques that correspond to the individual learning style and attitudes, might also be helpful.

Depending on the current learning environment, network members also require some technical skills to search for explicit information that is available on online resources, to handle a simulation system, or to navigate through the content of a learning platform.

Communication skills and the ability to work in teams are also critical for members of this network reference type, since learning not only takes place throughout an organization, but also in smaller groups within personal networks, which could also be subgroups within the learning network.

Network Leader. A network leader within a learning network will usually be considered an expert and will frequently play a teaching role. Often, he/she will serve as a moderator of the learning processes that are taking place. In the case of ICT-based forms of learning networks, the network leader/moderator needs the skills to perform this role in a virtual environment by using the appropriate ICT tools.

Organize the People and the Meetings

Organizing the knowledge network through public and private activities will help to develop a community.

Why this is important:

- Public activities such as conferences and workshops, as well as private person-to-person discussions with potential members and external experts, will develop a community whose members have a common purpose.
- These activities help members learn together through one another's experiences and allow for discussions that build strong relationships and help to improve capabilities.
- This helps members to accelerate their own professional development and to learn new insights and methods that can be applied to solve particular problems.

Think about it!

- There are different kinds of meetings, conferences and workshops that can be organized. Each of them has a special set of members and a special purpose.

- Regular meetings to discuss issues, build relationships, help one another with difficult problems, coordinate efforts, discuss extent of membership (who should be included and how to integrate them), and negotiate a learning agenda.
- An annual worldwide or company-wide conference of practitioners to share ideas, methods, stories, and results.
- Ongoing workshops with practitioners across business units who have common problems.
- Projects to identify, select, adapt, and maintain various types of content such as core documents, manuals, educational courses, etc.
- Education sessions (online and face-to-face) with internal and external experts on key topics.
- Core-group strategy sessions to identify recommendations and to address priorities across the company.

Steps to get you there:

1. Identify core-group members, conduct interviews, call informal contacts, identify the key issues for people with strong interests or needs (see step 4 in the roadmap).
2. Convene a group of potential core group members of the network to help develop the community.
3. Create a shared understanding of the purpose and function of the network.
4. Introduce members: who they are, areas of interest and expertise, their story of how they came to this network.
5. Identify common ground: what questions, needs and priorities are most important to the overall network?
6. Create a "network design" to build the practice and the community: time and agenda for meetings, specific projects to pursue, people to involve, etc.
7. Conduct public workshops or conferences to raise interest and awareness of the topic and to identify people with this interest and expertise.
8. Link the network with external experts, leading practitioners from other firms, and with internal groups (such as IT, HR, strategic

planning, training, and quality management) whose activities should be coordinated.

9. Assess and develop the community's ability to develop insights and tools over time, which are useful to apply in business units, and create a forum for professional development that attracts and challenges talented and willing contributors.

Facilitate Commitment of Members

The commitment of all network members is key in order to get the network up to speed and thus achieve a high performance.

Why this is important:

- Without commitment of the network members, the network will most likely have a low level of activity.
- This point is closely related to the step of "roles and responsibilities".

Think about it!

Commitment of the network members can be achieved by two means:

- Show and let the participants explicitly experience the benefits of the network, thus telling them why they should invest time in the network. Additionally, provide them with some type of intrinsic motivation (e.g., a certain prestige attached to being a member).
- Propose and define clear responsibilities and duties within the network which members have to acknowledge by signing an appropriate document. The demand to participate must come from top management and with a certain extrinsic motivation (e.g., one cannot afford not to be part of the network).

A combination of these two methods should be chosen. The intrinsic commitment might be used to initially attract people for the network, while the extrinsic commitment is useful to maintain the actual operation of the network.

Steps to get you there:

Intrinsic commitment:

- Create a vision to provide purpose and direction.
- Agree on core values.
- Develop a healthy climate to sustain the spirit within the network.
- Develop trust and mutual respect as the foundations of a knowledge network.
- Listen to, understand, and share with others.
- Create a sense of urgency and awareness of the benefits in order to get people to commit to, and allocate their time in favor of the network.
- Give rewards and provide incentives through recognition.

Extrinsic commitment:

- Use the list of responsibilities, tasks, and targets developed for the individual roles (see section "determine roles and responsibilities").
- Discuss the responsibilities, tasks, and targets with the network member assigned to the role.
- Have members sign the mutually agreed upon targets.
- Continually review targets and make assessments.
- This explicit outline of the different network members' tasks and duties also helps new network entrants when taking over a certain role from a predecessor, thus helping to gain their commitment.

Provide Organizational Tools to Create a Knowledge-enriching Environment and to Support People and Processes

Create a knowledge-enriching environment to support the on-going operation of the knowledge network. The following explanation applies to all network reference types.

Why this is important:

- Network leaders must know how to create a knowledge-enriching environment. With this, technological as well as human and organizational factors need to be considered.

Think about it!

- The possibility to create a knowledge-enriching environment is greatly dependent on the current organizational culture as a whole.

Steps to get you there:

1. Creating a knowledge-enriching environment is crucial for the success of all networks. Depending on the task that the network must carry out, a certain set of tools will be used for each specific knowledge network, in order to achieve a knowledge-enabling environment. For each tool a number of success factors exists, which should be considered in order to create an actual knowledge-enriching environment. In this case, we mainly speak of organizational tools.
2. A knowledge-enriching culture is characterized by:
   - an organizational climate of openness,
   - empowered individuals,
   - active learning (e.g., from the customer, and from the results of an individual's own actions),
   - a constant search for improvement and innovation,
   - intense, open, and widespread communications,
   - an organizational environment where one can experiment, reflect and learn,
   - boundary-crossing where individuals spend as much time interacting with those outside their network as with those within,
   - encouraging experimentation, rather than blindly following rules,
   - aligned goals and performance measures across departments, networks, and individuals,
   - willingness to share knowledge widely among colleagues, even those in different groups.

Organizational tools influencing the facilitating conditions and fostering a knowledge-enriching environment for:

Experiencing Network. The appropriate organizational tools have to be used in order to support specific characteristics of experiencing networks, and to foster a knowledge-enriching environment. The basis for choosing an appropriate tool is, again, the main operational knowledge task of transforming tacit knowledge into tacit knowledge that is pursued by these networks.

Since intensive communication between network members is crucial, communication tools are the most important tools to support experiencing networks. The following list gives an overview of relevant organizational tools that support an experiencing network:

- **Communication and coordination tools:**
  - knowledge forums
  - think-tanks
  - knowledge workshops
  - coffee corners/talk rooms
  - meeting and moderation tools
  - conversation and negotiation techniques
  - active listening
  - language tools (dialogue, story telling, common language, metaphors, controlled vocabulary, organizational thesaurus and dictionary)
- **Organization and management tools:**
  - management tools
    - conflict management tools
    - presentation techniques
    - HRM tools (e.g., job rotation, job enrichment, mentoring/coaching, training and development, and education)
    - knowledge vision/goals
    - contact/networking management
  - organizational structure tools
    - group work
    - roles and responsibilities (e.g., knowledge activists, community/network roles)
  - organizational culture tools
    - corporate culture change programs
    - organizational development tools
    - change agent

Materializing Network. Organizational tools in materializing networks must primarily support the process of transforming tacit knowledge into explicit knowledge. This process can be divided into two parts. First, tacit knowledge has to be identified and then articulated. Organizational tools to support this process are tools for visualization or language tools such as metaphors, analogies, etc. Furthermore, it should be emphasized that the process of articulating the knowledge is rather communication-intensive.

Second, the articulated knowledge has to be translated into an understandable format. Organizational tools may also support this task. Examples are organization and management tools such as presentation techniques, knowledge maps, defined roles and responsibilities in order to manage the process of bringing the knowledge into a well-structured and understandable format, etc.

The following list gives an overview of relevant organizational tools to support the knowledge reference mode materializing network:

- **Communication and coordination tools:**
  - knowledge forums
  - think-tanks
  - knowledge workshops
  - coffee corners/talk rooms
  - meeting and moderation tools
  - conversation and negotiation techniques
  - active listening
  - language tools (dialogue, story telling, common language, metaphors, controlled vocabulary, organizational thesaurus and dictionary)
- **Organization and management tools:**
  - management tools
    - presentation techniques
    - knowledge maps
    - visualization tools
    - knowledge vision/goals
  - organizational structure tools
    - roles and responsibilities (e.g., knowledge authors, reviewers, and content manager)
    - group work
    - project management
    - knowledge units
  - organizational culture tools
    - corporate culture change programs
    - organizational development tools
    - change agent

Resystematizing Network. A wide range of organizational tools exists to support the resystematizing network mode and influence the relevant knowledge work processes, the cultural and structural facilitating conditions, as well as network characteristics.

A number of organizational communication and coordination tools might be used for the particular exchange of explicit knowledge. In addition, organization and management tools help to manage knowledge work processes, to establish the network structure by providing roles, to influence the knowledge culture by using organizational culture tools, and so forth.

The following list gives an overview of relevant organizational tools for resystematizing networks:

- **Communication and coordination tools:**
  - knowledge forums
  - think-tanks
  - knowledge workshops
  - meeting and moderation tools
  - language tools (common language, metaphors, controlled vocabulary, organizational thesaurus and dictionary)
- **Organization and management tools:**
  - management tools
    - performance management tools
    - visualization tools (e.g., knowledge maps)
    - self-management tools
    - rewards and incentives
    - knowledge vision/goals
  - organizational structure tools
    - roles and responsibilities (e.g., knowledge gatherer, knowledge analyst, knowledge author, knowledge reviewer, and content manager)
    - knowledge units
  - organizational culture tools
    - corporate culture change programs
    - organizational development tools
    - change agent

Learning Network. Tools in learning networks primarily support the transformation of explicit knowledge into tacit knowledge. In this process at least two sub-processes have to be taken into account: first, explicit knowledge has to be made available in a suitable form (e.g., well structured, easily readable, and understandable, etc). Second, the explicit knowledge has to materialize through action and practice. Thus, close attention should be paid when selecting the particular organizational tools to support the special circumstances of explicit knowledge.

The following list offers a more comprehensive overview of organizational tools to support learning networks:

- **Communication and coordination tools:**
  - knowledge forums
  - think-tanks
  - knowledge workshops
  - meeting and moderation tools
  - language tools (common language, metaphors, controlled vocabulary, organizational thesaurus and dictionary)
- **Organization and management tools:**
  - management tools
    - performance management tools
    - visualization tools (e.g., presentation techniques, and knowledge maps)
    - scenario learning
    - simulation
    - planning tools (e.g., scenario techniques)
    - self-management tools (e.g., time management)
    - HRM tools (e.g., mentoring, coaching, and training and education)
    - learning tools (e.g., learning lessons, and learning journeys)
    - feedback
    - rewards and incentives
    - knowledge vision/goals
  - organizational structure tools
    - roles and responsibilities (e.g., network moderator, media expert, trainer, and coach)
    - group work
    - project management
    - organizational culture tools
    - corporate culture change programs
    - organizational development tools
    - change agent

Organize the Appropriate ICT Architecture

The operation of a knowledge network is also supported by a wide variety of ICT tools, which help to achieve the appropriate facilitating conditions. To support knowledge management in general, there are different knowledge technologies such as text mining, conceptual mapping, or intelligence agents. However, collaborative technologies, a category that includes groupware, intranets, videoconferencing, and document management, have delivered the most widespread benefits to knowledge practices.

The following steps describe how a knowledge base is set up for knowledge networks in general, followed by a description of certain technologies that are appropriate to support a certain network reference type.

However, for practitioners, there may be other important criteria to help decide which tools should be used, and these should therefore be carefully considered. These criteria are:

- Concrete usage/task or business case.
- Task of network (related to business goals).
- Existing ICT infrastructure.
- Business process orientation (loose/tight integration).
- Working conditions (e.g., are face-to-face meetings possible?).
- Skills of network members.
- Personal habits, habits within branch/company.
- Resource/time pressure.
- IT strategy.
- Cost.
- Organizational culture.

Set Up a Knowledge Base for All Network Types

Information and communication technology (ICT) tools support processes that help to fulfill the operational knowledge task and also influence, directly and/or indirectly, the network's facilitating conditions. The following discusses a knowledge base that is appropriate for all network reference types.

Why this is important:

- A knowledge base is a central element used to share knowledge within the community. The necessary effort by the community to develop the online resource is critical for its success. The development and application of practice resources depend largely on the strength of the network – its members will determine the priorities, what material to develop, and how effectively it is used.

- An important point is whether or not you have to create your own knowledge base for your network as an online resource. A knowledge base includes and integrates all sorts of explicit and tacit sources of knowledge, and possibly different types of knowledge systems (e.g., ERP systems, and groupware systems). Core documents, tools, methods, and courses that constitute the basic elements of the network practice are usually part of the knowledge base. Such a common platform or knowledge base helps to establish a network identity.

Think about it!

- The opportunities to use technology to feed the knowledge agenda are vast. Unfortunately, it is not easy to find a toolset that meets all needs. Standardization and integration are important topics that must be considered when choosing a toolset.
- A minimum goal with respect to which tools to use, might be to define at least one common tool for knowledge exchange.
- If different tools are used, it is important to define interfaces and formats for information exchange.

Steps to get you there:

1. Convene network members to agree on the overall purpose and function of the knowledge base.
2. Develop a mutual understanding of the range of types of practice documents and tools that will help practitioners.
3. Identify gaps and priorities in the knowledge base from the knowledge audit for the knowledge management practice.
4. Scan internally and externally to identify useful content that corresponds to each knowledge type from the list of practice elements

(e.g. articles and books, case studies, etc).

5. Select, adapt, and customize content for use.
6. Determine the design and functionality of the knowledge management practice website to help the community to store and access its practice resources; be sure to consider accessibility, feedback, search, communicate, design style, etc.
7. Market the value and possible uses of practice expertise to network members and other people who could benefit.
8. Ensure that the practice resource base is maintained and kept up-to-date as the community and its experience grow.

Experiencing Network ICT Tools. There are various ICT tools that are helpful in supporting knowledge networks of this type, particularly to overcome the geographical dispersal of an experiencing network's members. Examples of virtual communities demonstrate that establishing personal relationships, trust, and sharing experiences and tacit knowledge can, to some degree, be done "virtually" as well. Therefore, ICT communication tools (especially synchronous technologies and tools with a high degree of media richness) are mostly relevant for this network reference type, whereas intelligent tools, organization and management tools, as well as a knowledge base, are less important.

The following list gives an overview of relevant ICT tools to support the knowledge reference mode experiencing network:

- **Communication and coordination tools:**
  - messaging/e-mail
  - real-time conferencing systems
  - non-real-time conferencing systems (e.g., discussion databases)
  - learning platforms
  - community tools
- **Integration and database tools:**
  - i-net-technologies (some of them)
  - knowledge management suites

Materializing Network ICT Tools. Diverse database tools help provide a knowledge base in which explicit knowledge can be made accessible in a materializing network. Since this process can be structured quite well, the utilization of workflow management tools is also possible. Furthermore, some intelligence tools might be put in place, for example, skill mining tools to identify experts for certain content areas or problem-solving tools such as reasoning technologies.

The following list gives an overview of relevant organizational and ICT tools to support the reference mode materializing network:

- **Communication and coordination tools:**
  - messaging/e-mail
  - workflow management
  - group decision support systems
  - real-time conferencing systems
  - non-real-time conferencing systems (e.g., discussion databases)
  - learning platforms
  - community tools
- **Organization and management tools:**
  - visualization tools
  - creativity tools
- **Intelligence tools:**
  - skill mining
  - categorization/clustering
  - problem solving tools
- **Integration and database tools:**
  - i-net-technologies (some of them)
  - knowledge management suites
  - databases
  - data dictionaries
  - repositories

Resystematizing Network ICT Tools. In resystematizing networks, nearly all the potential provided by ICT can be utilized. In other words, not only the communication in knowledge networks and closely related knowledge tasks such as locating/capturing, sharing/transferring, or storing knowledge can be supported electronically, but also tasks to manage and control the network, such as measurement and performance management. The use of intelligence tools, specifically "intelligence agents" which are to a certain degree able to act autonomously, might lead to an understanding of knowledge networks in which software systems not only play a role as tools, but rather, similar to the human representatives, become autonomous actors.

The following list gives an overview of relevant organizational and ICT tools for resystematizing networks:

- **Communication and coordination tools:**
    - document management/archiving
    - workflow management
    - messaging/e-mail
    - calendaring/scheduling
    - real-time conferencing systems (video conferencing, audio conferencing, and data conferencing (chat, whiteboard, and application sharing))
    - non-real-time conferencing systems (e.g., discussion databases)
    - learning platforms
    - group editing/group document handling
    - community tools
    - collaborative filtering
    - CSCW-suites
- **Organizational and management tools:**
    - personal information management (PIM)
    - decision support systems
    - management support systems/executive support systems
    - visualization tools
    - creativity tools
    - measuring tools
- **Intelligence tools:**
    - intelligence agents
    - data mining
    - text mining
    - business intelligence
    - categorization/clustering tools
    - problem solving tools (neural networks, reasoning, and rule-based systems)
- **Integration and database tools:**
    - i-net-technologies
    - CSCW/groupware-suites
    - knowledge management suites
    - enterprise portals
    - databases
    - data dictionaries
    - repositories
    - data warehousing
    - search and retrieval

Learning Network ICT Tools. There is a wide range of ICT tools to support the facilitating conditions of a learning network in order to provide access to explicit knowledge for learning purposes. Learning platforms, visualization tools, learning portals, audio and video streaming, and community tools are just a few of them. After obtaining access to explicit knowledge, the second process of embodying the explicit knowledge – in which communication plays an important role – might be supported with organizational and ICT tools as well. Examples of organizational tools are various communication tools and also organization and management tools such as coaching, mentoring, simulation, scenario learning, group work, and project management. ICT tools with which to support this process entail the entire tool class of synchronous and asynchronous communication tools, tools for personal information management (PIM), simulation and modeling tools, and so forth.

As with the other network reference type, organizational tools also exist to influence cultural aspects within learning networks. The goal, therefore, should be to establish a knowledge culture that encourages the desired learning processes.

The following list gives a more comprehensive overview of ICT tools with which to support learning networks:

- **Communication and coordination tools:**
  - messaging/e-mail
  - real-time conferencing systems (video conferencing, audio conferencing, and data conferencing (chat, whiteboard, and application sharing))
  - non-real-time conferencing systems (e.g., discussion databases)
  - learning platforms
  - community tools
- **Organizational and management tools:**
  - personal information management (PIM)
  - scheduling/calendaring
  - simulation and modeling tools
  - visualization tools
- **Integration and database tools:**
  - i-net technologies
  - knowledge management suites
  - enterprise portals
  - databases
  - repositories
  - search and retrieval

However, ICT tools not only serve to facilitate the capturing, transferring and creating of explicit and tacit knowledge, but can also serve as a connection to the outside world. By establishing a platform for relationships, appropriate ICT tools can help communicate the aims, aspirations, and goals of a particular knowledge network to other parts of the company, other customers, or other stakeholders. The facilitation of relationships to the outside world will be elaborated on in the next section.

5.5.3 Facilitate Relationships to the Outside World

The aim of this section is to elaborate on the connections the network has to the outside world. It is, on one hand, an attempt to define the boundaries of the network, and, on the other hand, an attempt to achieve continuous support and understanding from people not involved in the network by presenting the benefits of the knowledge network.

In the first part of this section, a knowledge management board is developed in order to keep an eye on the company's strategic direction. Second, a broker is brought in to provide the knowledge network with the necessary support from the outside. Third, and very critical, the coordination and integration with other functions have to be thought through in order solve problems such as the network members' rival tasks.

The outcome of this section should be a sound relationship between the network and the outside world, which does not isolate the network, but supports the network to get its tasks done.

Develop the Knowledge Management Board

The knowledge management board is a group of people who support the knowledge network and help to assess its knowledge. It is not, however, equivalent to the company's knowledge management board of directors. The purpose of the knowledge board is to give strategic direction to provide the focus and level of investment in knowledge management and network-development activities, and to provide influence when and where needed to ensure the effectiveness of these investments.

Why is this important:

- The knowledge management department should provide the board with status reports on knowledge management initiatives as well as analyses of the impact of these initiatives on strategic objectives. The knowledge management department should also recommend ways in which the board can help to influence policies in HR and IT to respond to business-unit needs and to improve coordination between knowledge management initiatives and related quality management, process improvement, and restructuring efforts.

- The board helps the knowledge management department keep knowledge management initiatives credible, focused, and appropriately funded by knowing what is going on and by sanctioning the knowledge management department to coordinate knowledge management efforts for the entire company.

Think about it!

Typical activities of the knowledge management board:

- Meets every 3-6 months for 2-4 hours to review knowledge management initiatives.
- Knowledge management activities: What activities are underway? How are they aligned with corporate or business-unit strategies and objectives? Are they on target with regard to milestones, resources, and impact?
- Company-wide themes and challenges: What cross-business-unit or cross-functional issues are there and what are the priorities? What are the knowledge management department recommendations for addressing them?
- Reviews the emerging strategic priorities and how knowledge management approaches can help to strengthen the analysis and execution of strategies.
- Knowledge management impact: What are the results of knowledge management investments at the corporate and business-unit levels? What have we learned? What are the recommendations for acting on the lessons learned?
- Evaluate the board's own actions and consider what additional or different types of influence or support are needed from corporate senior management as well as act appropriately to add or change board functions or members.
- Evaluate and provide guidance for the overall strategy and budget of knowledge management functions.

Steps to get you there:

1. Develop the knowledge management board's vision: what types of support or influence may be required to implement the knowledge management strategy as it is currently understood:
   - support from business units,
   - support from HR, IT, and other functions,
   - access to resources,
   - increase visibility and senior managers' understanding of the power of knowledge management approaches,
   - influence relevant policies such as performance appraisals and information system choices,
   - sanction the leadership role for the knowledge management department.
2. Define appropriate criteria to select knowledge management board members:
   - key divisions, functions (e.g., line & staff) and levels are represented,
   - informal and formal power in the company,
   - interest in knowledge management,
   - alignment with knowledge management vision and values,
   - availability.
3. Conduct formal interviews as well as informal networking to understand senior management's interests and priorities, to educate them about knowledge management elements and strategies, and to identify appropriate members for an effective knowledge management board.
4. Facilitate selection of the initial knowledge management board members and convene its first meeting, which should focus on four issues:
   - develop a shared understanding of the company strategy (business goals), and how knowledge management activities and strategy support it,
   - define how the board will support the knowledge management strategy,

- negotiate clear expectations of how the knowledge management department will work together with the board to fulfill its role.

5. Review the current state of knowledge management initiatives in the company and show how the knowledge management strategy responds to specific gaps and opportunities.

Provide or Broker Support to Internal Network Initiatives

If there is an increasing number of knowledge management and network initiatives across your company, there should be a knowledge management department in which these activities can be organized and supported.

Why this is important:

- It should adopt a networking approach, thus brokering services among a network of providers and clients.

Think about it!

- The knowledge management department should develop sufficient internal capabilities to help business units accurately interpret their needs and find the right type of help to respond to these needs.
- The knowledge management department should be positioned to identify key issues across business units, help evaluate and select appropriate education and consulting resources, and assess which methods and external partners are most effective and why.
- Typical ways in which the knowledge management department can support business units include:
  - as a consultant to business-unit senior management and knowledge management leaders to help them interpret how knowledge management challenges relate to the business-unit strategy and performance objectives,
  - developing a network of consultation and education experts on a variety of topics related to knowledge management and knowledge networks as part of its ongoing participation in an external knowledge management community,

- brokering contacts and helping to negotiate contracts with a range of consulting and education resources based on the specific needs and preferences of business-unit clients,
- consulting internal business-unit clients on topics on which the knowledge management department members have developed specific expertise,
- helping clients take advantage of resources in the knowledge management practice resource base, and to leverage the knowledge of expert practitioner members of the knowledge network.

Steps to get you there:

1. Build a department with knowledge management experts, give them the potency to act, and position them in a central place in your company. Make sure that they know what they have to do.
2. To support knowledge management initiatives, identify the needs of the business-unit internal clients and stakeholders through formal interviews, informal networking, and the ongoing activities of the knowledge network (conferences, workshops, core-group meetings, etc).
3. Organize a network of external experts who can provide consultation and education for business-unit clients as part of participation in an external knowledge network.
4. Form a partnership with external experts to consult and educate internal business-unit clients to build expertise, to help them internalize and customize knowledge for your company, and to assess and enhance the effectiveness of external partners.
5. Develop a strategic plan that identifies the types and depths of the knowledge management development needs, the segments of internal clients, the calculations of the required resources (internal and external), and the proposed impact thereof on the business.
6. Convene community members to agree on the overall purpose and functions of a resource base for knowledge management practice.
7. Develop a shared understanding of the range of types of practice documents and tools that will help practitioners as described in the proposed list above.

8. Identify gaps and priorities in the knowledge base for the knowledge management practice.
9. Scan internally and externally to identify useful content that corresponds to each "knowledge type" in the list of practice elements (e.g., articles and books, case studies, etc).
10. Select, adapt, and customize content for use in the knowledge network.
11. Determine the design and functionality of the knowledge management practice website to help the community store and access its practice resources. Consider accessibility, feedback, search, communication, design style, etc.
12. Market the value and possible uses of practice expertise to network members and other persons who could benefit.
13. Ensure that the practice resource base is maintained and kept up-to-date as the community and its practice grow.

Integrate and Coordinate with Other Functions

There are a number of units and functional groups whose work influences or overlaps the functions associated with the network activities.

Why this is important:

- Some are needed to support knowledge management initiatives (like HR or IT).
- Some produce information or deal with issues that are related to the work of knowledge networks (like QM, process improvement and error prevention).
- The knowledge management department should help to educate senior management, help staff groups to understand how knowledge management initiatives relate to them, and then provide options and recommendations for ways to enhance performance in these areas by applying knowledge management and knowledge network approaches.

Think about it!

Typical integration and coordination activities may include:

- Formal interviews and informal networking with senior, functional, and staff managers to understand their needs and priorities, educate them on knowledge management applications and approaches, and together consider recommendations for better integration or coordination.

- Specific projects to improve integration, such as co-leading a project team, to develop a performance appraisal that reinforces knowledge development, to co-develop an executive development course on knowledge management, or to help senior managers consider informal and formal structural options for competing in emerging markets.
- Help link staff and functional groups to external best practices, such as McKinsey & Company's human resource practices or British Petroleum's technology-based learning methods.
- Discussions with the knowledge management board about integration opportunities – both fulfilled and missed – and appropriate actions to take (see above "discussion of the board").

Steps to get you there:

1. Conduct interviews and informal networking with senior, functional, and staff managers to assess needs and priorities and to discuss action options.
2. Develop standardized interview templates for staff functions.
3. Identify high-potential projects with specific staff or functional groups in which increased integration is likely to succeed and to have a high impact.
4. Create a reporting format to review the status of the knowledge management coordination and integration efforts with the knowledge management board. Prepare the initial recommendations to improve the integration for the first knowledge management board meeting.

5.5.4 Establish Internal Measurement

This section serves to identify the potential means to internally measure the performance of a network and how to establish these means. These measurements set the foundation for the following section "measure and adapt".

The choice of the appropriate incentives, as well as the appropriate awards presented in the initial part, is the first step to measurement. Incentives and rewards have the potential to steer the behavior of the network in favor of the network performance. Second, the degree of the achievement of the targets of the individual or the role, as well as the network as a whole, has to be evaluated and overall measures established. Third, the key success factors for each individual network will help to identify whether the knowledge network is successful or not and to determine where action should take place.

Choose and Organize the Appropriate Rewards/Incentives

The appropriate reward and incentive systems depend on the company culture and are therefore very specific. But, there are some issues that apply to every company in its motivation of network members to engage in the network.

Why this is important:

- A frequent barrier to better knowledge sharing is an inappropriate reward system. Employees must be motivated to spend time in developing and sharing their knowledge and therefore work in the knowledge network. Many companies are now making knowledge contributions part of each individual's annual appraisal and pay award. The benchmarks to reach and the measures to show the efforts are different (see the next step) and depend on the company culture, but there are some important issues that apply to all companies and networks.
- The appraisal system of the company must consider knowledge work and therefore commitment to a network to demonstrate to employees that their work is of a certain value to the company.

Think about it!

- *Intrinsic* rewards are as important as *monetary* rewards. But, take into account that monetary incentives are only short-term motivators. Regularly scheduled monetary incentives can become a counter-productive factor.

- Consider which activities you want to support. If you want to support a better cooperation, choose *team incentives.* If an individual shall be rewarded, you should choose *individual incentives* or rewards, but this could be counter-productive if the other members of the network do not agree with an exception being made of only one person in a team.
- Set clear criteria for achieving a reward and/or incentive and communicate these to everybody involved.
- Reward quality before quantity.
- Various forms of *recognition* are needed. These include complimenting and praising individuals for their contributions, and giving them opportunities for external visibility and recognition through presentations and publications.
- Take into account that motivation can also be provided through the assignment of specific tasks, visibility as an expert, a presentation to the top management, or training.
- Annual awards for knowledge achievement are also motivators. A more tangible incentive is a stake in the future prosperity of the business.
- Small networks might not use any reward systems at all. Within a group of only a few people, another mechanism to enhance commitment and collaboration comes into play. This could be a more tacit-like incentive system of social rewards and mutual recognition, since official rewards could have a negative effect on the group performance. Those small networks' incentives are more likely to be non-monetary incentives.
- Large knowledge networks might have a balanced relation between monetary and non-monetary incentives.

Steps to get you there:

1. Differentiate between what you want to reward or which person you want to motivate, the engagement of the individual, the optimal fulfillment of a role in the network, or the cooperation in the network – ultimately, the work of the network.

2. Choose the appropriate reward or incentives in line with the company culture. In all companies the use of specific incentives/rewards for the individual, role, and team is normal. Choose a reward/incentive from these.

Establish Measures for the Individual/Role/Network

Assess the impact of the knowledge network on the achievement of the business goals risk reduction, efficiency improvement, and increased innovation.

Why this is important:

Measuring the impact is important for:

- Justification of the knowledge network approach.
- Optimal allocation of resources within the company, and for ultimately judging whether the network is high performing or not.

Think about it!

- The impact of knowledge management initiatives has to be assessed across the company. Assessments should be both systematic and sufficiently sensitive to the dynamic nature and social aspects of knowledge management in action. This provides valid and useable results. It is impossible to assess the true impact of knowledge management and to identify useful lessons learned without the committed involvement of the knowledge workers who build, share, and apply the knowledge.

Typical activities related to assessing knowledge management impact include:

- Develop, renew, and customize methods and tools for assessing networks.
- Work with business-unit knowledge management leaders to create assessment methods that are aligned with their performance and learning objectives.
- Cooperate with external experts and leading practitioners from other firms to develop and learn to apply assessment methods that work.

- Conduct assessments (with the help of external partners) for corporate and business-unit level knowledge management initiatives and assist in creating reports for internal clients.
- Report the overall results of knowledge management initiatives to the knowledge management board and recommend appropriate actions.

Other important issues that have to be considered are:

- Developing a generic approach for assessing knowledge management impact that can be applied to knowledge domains and networks for use by managers at the corporate, network, and individual level.
- Identifying the initial areas for the application and testing of assessment methods.
- Reviewing results and lessons learned in terms of both, knowledge management and the assessment process itself – incorporate insights and adapt tools and methodologies.
- Applying validated assessment methods on demand for internal clients; and on the corporate level for reporting to the knowledge management board.
- Using analysis data as basis for publications in academic and business press – as well as internal presentations – to help educate people on and influence their understanding of knowledge management approaches and impact.

Steps to get you there:

Measurement of the individual, role, and network activities is directly derived from the indicators of the knowledge network scorecard. In order to have a successful measurement system, one should follow certain steps:

- Develop a greater *awareness and understanding* of the role of knowledge and the nature of intellectual capital.
- Create a *common language* that is more widely diffused within the company, e.g., using terms such as "human capital".
- Identify *indicators* that are suitable and appropriate, and develop a

measurement model that encloses these indicators in a coherent framework.

- Introduce *measurement systems,* including the accompanying management processes, that guide and reward managers.

Success Factors

In this section we describe knowledge networks' success factors according to their ideal characteristics. The following lists the extent to which each characteristic will help to identify whether the knowledge network is successful or not, and to deduce where action should take place.

Checkbox: Success Factors for Experiencing Networks

- Narrow personal relationships (which correspond to "strong ties" in network analysis) to create a climate of trust and to support the actual exchange of tacit knowledge through personal contact.
- A rather small network size.
- Common activities, and face-to-face contact.
- A knowledge enriching culture.
- Closeness.
- Advanced communication requirements.
- A potential high degree of media richness and the support potential of the communication and coordination tools.

Checkbox: Success Factors for Materializing Networks

- Knowledge culture that provides values such as care, trust, and openness.
- High communication requirements such as techniques with which to express one's ideas.
- A knowledge base should be developed and used.
- A well-structured network, since the process of translating knowledge into an understandable form can be subdivided into different roles such as knowledge authors, and reviewers.

- The communication and coordination tools are intensively used for support.

Checkbox: Success Factors for Resystematizing Networks

- The knowledge network must have a distinct structure.
- The knowledge itself must be in a structured and codified form.
- There must be a common knowledge base of some type.
- ICT tools should be supported.
- Organizational tools and management tools should be supported.
- The knowledge should be less bound to a specific context and therefore easier to transfer.
- The network can be large and the geographical dispersal of resystematizing networks can be rather wide.
- There has to be a knowledge culture of some sort, since the exchange of explicit knowledge might suffer if such a culture is lacking.

Checkbox: Success Factors for Learning Networks

Identification and understanding of the explicit knowledge:

- The knowledge itself must be in a structured and codified form.
- There must be a common knowledge base of some type.
- ICT tools should be supported appropriately.
- Communication tools are quite important for the support of the learning process.

The process of embodying the knowledge:

- Personal relationships.
- Face-to-face-contacts.
- Geographical and social proximity.
- A training and mentoring program.

Learning Case

Where should Merlin start with setting up of the network now that she has identified the exact goals and needs, as well as the appropriate network reference type? And whom should she contact about the needs, achievements, and the goals of the network? When should she do this? She draws up a communication plan for the top management, for the people involved in the start-up, as well as for the individual/potential members. Furthermore, she develops the key mission, values, and benefits of the network as deduced from the knowledge audit.

First she has to communicate her intention to the top management in order to obtain their commitment. As soon as this has been acquired, she wants to get more people involved. But the hardest part is to convince top management of her idea of setting up a knowledge network. Even though Merlin has already tried to motivate some key managers for the issue (after all, they contacted her in the first place and made her aware of the problem), she also really wants to recruit sponsors to support the project financially. She therefore needs to communicate her exact strategy and goals. She maps her findings from the previous analysis, namely the potential to leverage the developers' local knowledge for these potential sponsors, and makes concrete suggestions as to how the knowledge network could support these. Even though there are other priorities on the top management's agenda, they agree to her project because they also see an opportunity to leverage the first knowledge network experience in another area.

Now that she has the go-ahead from top-management, Merlin starts to identify what the intermediate tasks and goals of the network are going to be. The task will be for selected specialists from the material treatment teams to have regular meetings, in order to exchange knowledge on a clearly defined area, for example, the different testing methods, or how to set up material treatment processes. The designated goal of the network will be to increase the rate of innovation overall. She and the already identified key experts agree on the key content needed for the achievement of the goals, as well as specifying what skills and competencies are needed in the network.

The goals, tasks, and activities have to be made visible as well. To do so, she invites the key material specialists, potential knowledge network members, and Patrick H., who she thinks could be a good network leader, to a workshop. In this small workshop they will together define the needed roles and responsibilities, the goals and targets, as well as draw up a list of possible concrete tasks to act upon, such as the writing and completion of a handbook by the end of the following year to harmonize the work in the different material treatment areas with different instruments.

Now that the network exists as a project, Merlin wants to bring life into the network – to involve people more, to obtain their commitment to participate and thus facilitate the relationships within the network. Therefore, the next important step for her is to identify the network's participants and to organize the first meeting. After all, now that the network has started she wants to withdraw and simply serve as a consultant to the network.

She now needs to get an acknowledged expert with a high degree of social skills (e.g., to facilitate care and trust in the network) who has the ability and responsibility to facilitate the communication of the network, and who can be a moderator, motivator and representative of the network. And who would also take over the project. Merlin decides to assign the key role of the network leader to Patrick H., an acknowledged senior material specialist, who has considerable experience in leading projects. In addition, he is accepted and respected by most of the other specialists at SoundSource.

Another explicit role she needs to fill is that of a "knowledge editor" who reformats conversations, emails and other unstructured knowledge into more structured knowledge. Someone else has to fill the role of a "content expert" or "book owner", i.e. someone who is the main contact person for a specific content area. At a global conference a content expert is identified for each country. Different subgroups meetings are also convened in order to decide on the means for interacting and to get to know each other. After finding the appropriate people to interact in the network, Merlin organizes meetings to plot maps of the special responsibilities and the associated tasks in the network. The participants come to an agreement and show their commitment by signing it. This map will also make it easier to involve new members in the network, since it outlines the tasks and responsibilities for them.

But how should network members mutually identify their tacit knowledge and capture it? What should the process of sharing and developing knowledge among the members be like? They use the functional map of a materializing network to obtain a generic overview of the processes that have to be organized and discuss them with the network participants.

In order to get these members up to speed, to exchange their knowledge and experience, and thus bring the network to life, Merlin and Patrick must work on facilitating a knowledge-enriching environment. This means that the network's activities have to be supported by appropriate organizational tools, which in a materializing network, primarily assist the process of transforming tacit knowledge into explicit knowledge. This process can be divided into two parts. First, the tacit knowledge of the material treatment of those different instruments has to be identified and then articulated. Organizational tools that can support this process are, for example, tools for visualization, or language tools such as metaphors, analogies, etc. Furthermore, the process of articulating knowledge is rather communication-intensive.

Second, the articulated knowledge has to be translated into an understandable format so that specialists, who work on another instrument with different materials, understand it as well. This task could also be supported with organizational tools. For example, presentation techniques or knowledge maps, in order to manage the process of presenting the knowledge in a well-structured and understandable format.

What ICT architecture should be chosen to support the work of the network? The members were, of course, using email regularly in order to exchange news or arrange meetings. But what else, if anything at all? The network members agree to use creativity tools for their meetings, and to develop a learning platform, as well as to set up a database that is guarded and maintained by specific people to prevent the occurrence of an information dump.

While setting up the internal operation of the network, the external relationships must also be established. A knowledge management board supports the knowledge network and helps assess its knowledge. Merlin is one of the knowledge managers communicating the task and goals of the network at different meetings throughout the company. She sends regular emails that inform all employees of the network and communicates this in several workshops as well.

One of the last important activities for Merlin and the network leader is to establish measurements. They discuss appropriate measurements for the individual, role, and network, and decide to establish concrete measurements for personal targets, depending on a person's task within the network (this task will be further elaborated on in the section "measure and adapt"). To motivate people to contribute to the network and to reward this, Merlin and the network leader plan to reward team developers who have contributed substantially to the network with tickets to the New Year Concert in Vienna. Nevertheless, the contribution would have to be substantial and useful. Monetary rewards are not favored because there is a danger of losing the participant's motivation after a while, and because it is not the company's custom to use money to motivate people.

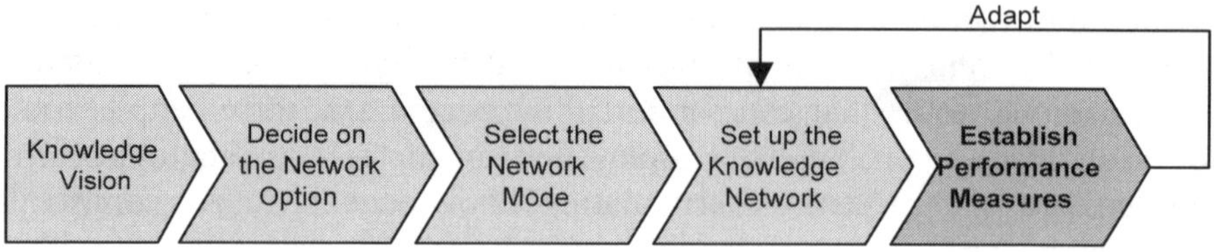

5.6 Measure and Adapt the Knowledge Network

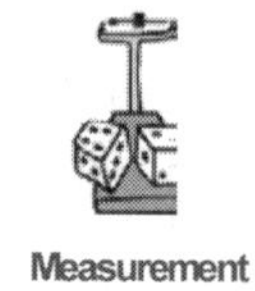

The measurement system that is presented in this handbook can be categorized by two main elements: the "internal" measurement system and the "external" measurement system for knowledge networks. The following figure provides an overview of the entire measurement system as it is presented in this handbook.

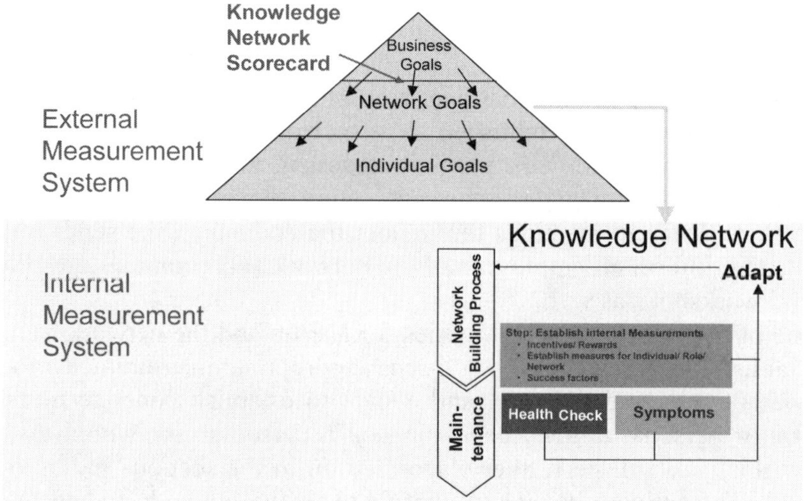

Fig. 34. Building blocks of the knowledge network measurement system

We begin with the "external" measurement system which is primarily comprised of the knowledge network scorecard (for detailed information see the section "building blocks" in this handbook) and the verification of the network option (for deeper insights see the corresponding section in the appendix of this handbook).

The knowledge scorecard is used to translate the business goals from company level to network level. Thereafter, a specific task or process is selected for execution by the network in order to achieve the relevant business goal. Thus, on a network level, one can determine whether the process or the task is being completed appropriately, and to what degree it contributes to the achievement of the business goals.

To have a comprehensive measurement system, it is necessary to take a look into the knowledge network itself. The "internal" measurement system is therefore comprised of the health check and the symptoms of an ailing network - two independent measurement possibilities that determine the performance of the network. Their purpose is to measure whether the network operates correctly. They neither provide answers to whether the network option was the appropriate one to start with, nor to whether the task or process that the network executes is the correct one in respect of the chosen business goal.

The health check can best be performed directly after the network has been established in order to determine whether everything has been carried out correctly and efficiently. It should also be carried periodically to determine if the network is still operating according to the requirements. From these perspectives, it serves as a prophylactic function, and does not mention or analyze illness symptoms. In addition, not only efficiency, but also effectiveness has to be taken into account.

The symptoms of an ailing network can be analogously explained with reference to the human body: when somebody does not feel well, one has to determine the cause. Like-wise, if you have failures that pertain to a knowledge network's characteristics, an adaptation might be necessary. The symptoms help to determine the failures and facilitate the finding of an appropriate cure.

Both measurement methods include adaptation possibilities. If it is not worth changing or not worth adapting the network, then the only remaining option might be to let it die (see the section "fading and dying with grace").

5.6.1 Internal Knowledge Network Measurement System

A Health Check for the Knowledge Network

Is the performance of the knowledge network in line with the goals of the company? One way of answering this question is to examine some symptoms of an ailing network. Another way is to test the performance alignment of the knowledge network by using the health check discussed in the following section.

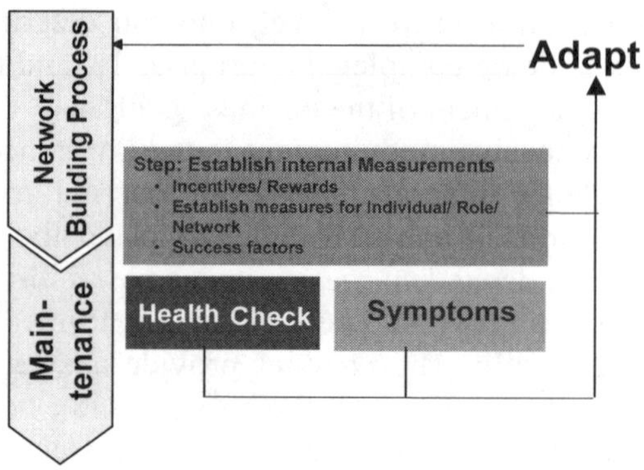

Fig. 35. Internal measurement system

The health check demonstrates how the performance of the network can be viewed from the network perspective, and how specific outcomes can be linked to concrete actions in order to achieve improvements. Starting with the network perspective, one can also view the overriding issues on a company level. This health check is aimed to complement the knowledge scorecard that we have already introduced, in order to capture some prevailing coordination issues that cannot be measured by a scorecard. The health check also aims to incorporate some of the measurements of the scorecard, linking the outcomes to actions that have been taken in order to achieve the desired result.

If you are able to answer all of the questions on one level in the positive, you can move to the next level. If there are also negative answers look at the relevant page and adapt.

Where Is the Gap?

Start-up

- Is the network supported by the top management? Is it accepted?
- Is the strategy communicated clearly to the top management, the relevant people such as stakeholders, the entire company and the potential/involved members?
- Did the network receive the appropriate support in respect of resources, such as time, attention, people, and money?
- Did the network members work on a specific task or activity? Did the network fulfill a concrete goal derived from a specific business goal?
- Did every member know what specific task he/she has to fulfill in the network? Did everybody know the concrete processes that have to be executed to solve the network's operational knowledge task?

- Is the output of the knowledge work processes such that the next process in line can be started?

→ **No: see section 5.5.1**

↓

Facilitate relationships within the network

- Are the roles and responsibilities clearly defined? Does everybody know which responsibilities are attached to each role? Is it clear who the participants in the network are? Do people know each other?
- Are the people sufficiently organized by the network leader? Are the meetings organized well?
- Do the network members show the necessary commitment? Does the network leader support this commitment?
- Are the appropriate organizational tools provided in order to support the network's knowledge creation efforts?
- Is the appropriate ICT architecture in place to support the network's operational knowledge task? Are there communication problems associated with the ICT infrastructure?

→ **No: see section 5.5.2**

↓

Facilitate relationships with the outside world

- Is a knowledge management board in place? Does it actively support the network in its activities? Does it provide it with strategic guidance? Does the board improve the effectiveness of the network?
- Does the company have a knowledge management department that supports the network activities? Does the knowledge management department provide the network with the necessary information to pursue its tasks, for example, about other knowledge management activities in the company?
- Are other company functions integrated in the network that have a reciprocal influence on the work of the network? Are there conflicts to be resolved?

→ **No: see section 5.5.3**

↓

Establish measurements

- Are the appropriate rewards and incentives in place to motivate an individual or a team? Are they in line with the company culture?
- Is the performance of the individual, the role, and the network evaluated appropriately? Are network goals included in the personal goal system? Does the network leader look after role fulfillment and does he provide feedback?
- Is the performance of the network periodically evaluated – internally as well as externally (using the health check, symptoms of failure and the KNN – scorecard)? Is there a specific scorecard in place that translates the business goals into network goals? Did the network members participate in this process?
- Are they familiar with the goals? Is the fulfillment of the network goals apparent to the responsible managers?

→ **No: see section 5.5.4**

Symptoms of an Ailing Network

Having identified failures/mistakes that can occur within networks, as well as disadvantageous variables that cannot be directly influenced by the networks, the signals and symptoms of failure will now receive attention.
In the following we provide some key signals/symptoms of failures:

Task orientation/ roles of members:

- The network is not dynamic.
- The network is not fast.
- No resources given to the network.
- No/few deliveries or low quality of delivery.

Skills/experience:

- Indecisive leadership.

Relationships:

- Mistrust.
- No care is given to the network and network members by the leader.
- Frustration of the network members.

Benefit/value of members:

- No evaluation of results/deliverables.

- Uneven contribution of the network members in relation to the network activities.
- No enthusiasm, and initiative.

Shared objectives, aims, and interests:
- Meetings turn into conflicts.
- No common language.
- No common rituals.
- No common values.

Communication style, and media richness:
- Lack of communication in the network.
- No/limited communication.
- Unfocused communication.
- Lack of discipline in communication.

Identification, commitment, and multi-membership:
- Vision and purpose of the network are constantly being questioned
- Few/less people come to network meetings.
- Too little time is spent on participation/network activities.
- The people involved are being lost.
- Successes are not celebrated.

Boundaries, knowledge access, and openness:
- No links (of the network) to other parts of the organization.
- Feeling of disconnectedness.
- Little/less input of information/knowledge/work.
- Different unintended subgroups in the network.
- Faction forming is occurring.
- No thought process occurring.

Size, geographical closeness, and formalization:
- No regular meetings.
- Network center is ignored.

In the following, actions for handling or avoiding failures within and outside of networks will be described. The proposed measures will again be related to the dimensions/characteristics, as well as the environment, the organizational embedding, and the support level to indicate how to react in the case of special problems/ failures (see below).

Table 17. Potential steps and their adaptation regarding network failures

Failures related to:	Adaptation:
Task orientation/ roles of members	Linking networks to organizational goals and projects and making this link evident Giving the network a clearly described and formal status Making the network visible to the organization Communicating deliverables, activities, and impact of networks on the business areas Defining network tasks as an official part of the job tasks, and defining clear performance aspirations Defining the priority of the network tasks regarding other job tasks, Defining clear responsibilities/role activities Bringing in a new leader if needed Ascertaining that the network leader will ensure progress, openness and learning
Skills/ experience	Identifying and selecting people carefully Bringing in new people every time this is needed Clarifying people's personal goal/interest in participation Providing training/development
Relationships	Defining a social contract that describes the way of working, mutual respect, trust, etc Organizing social activities Ensuring that the leader emphasizes networking-building activities
Benefit/value of members	Introducing a system for recognition and incentives Clarifying what is expected of and can be provided for the individual member, for the network, and for the organization
Shared objectives, aims, and interests	Not having too many sensitive topics simultaneously Defining specific objectives/targets/deliverables for the network Clearly prioritizing the objectives to pursue Setting clear performance aspirations
Communication style, and media richness	Having (more) physical/face-to-face meetings Introducing a knowledge scout Defining the way and frequency of "minimum" communication Using well-known and well-used communication means when possible

Table 17. Potential steps and their adaptation regarding network failures (continued)

Identification, commitment, and multi-membership	Reviews by the network leader to ensure progress, commitment, and initiative Celebrating successes and important results Providing the network with space to find its own identity
Boundaries, knowledge access, and openness	Ensuring that new people with own opinions are brought in
Size, geographical closeness, and formalization	Defining the way of working Defining procedures and the networks' regulation mechanisms Finalizing terms of reference Introducing/defining instruments to judge the network activities' functioning

Whereas the network itself or network members can make use of the actions above, this is not the case for the failures/mistakes associated with the environment, the organizational embedding, and the support level of the network.

Table 18. Potential action steps regarding failures/mistakes outside the network

Symptoms in the Network Environment	Possible adaptation
• No internal reason for existence • Too much pressure on networks; network members and organization have no patience • Lack of time for network members to participate • Not enough financial support for the network • No endorsement and continual support by the senior executives; no sponsorship	• Linking networks to organizational goals and projects, and providing the network with adequate status • Communicating the logic as well as the deliverables, activities, and the impact of networks on the business areas • Giving the network enough time to become established and to work • Providing the network with space to find its identity and its workings • Providing networks with experiences from other networks

Table 18. Potential action steps regarding failures/mistakes outside the network (continued)

• Results/findings of networks are not used/no tangible outputs	• Providing the network with financial resources, as well as with time that can be used for network activities • Defining network tasks as an official part of the job description • Being supporters/facilitators both in the network and in management in order to obtain needed resources • Introducing a system for recognition and incentives • Ensure that the network's results and experiences will be used in other areas as well • Introducing/defining instruments to judge the progress of the network activities

Fading and Dying with Grace

Networks with a decreasing activity level and registering a poor performance during a health check might decide to end their activities. However, both the phases of the decreasing activity level, as well as the possible "dying" of the network, should be closely managed. You could additionally consider the network's rebirth.

Why this is important:

- Even if a network is not built around a common task that has to be fulfilled, but around a common theme, its lifecycle can end.
- A network's topic might no longer be relevant; thus, the members and/or the management's commitment decreases.

Think about it!

- The network may be looking for a new orientation, a new subject, or new topics that question its whole identity.
- This phase may be associated with wistful feelings by and fond memories of its members.

- Resignation, disappointment, and/or conflicts may also arise.
- If a new network is going to be established, it is key to use the existing structure and knowledge in some way.

Steps to get you there:

1. Look for symptoms; monitor the development and action level of the network.
2. Make those symptoms explicit; communicate the decreasing action level and discuss it.
3. Envisage scenarios: let it fade or give the network a new task and thus let it be reborn.
4. Involve all the relevant people in the ultimate decision,.
5. If you decide to let the knowledge network fade, give awards for achievements and document the successes and the leanings.
6. Involve people in new projects.
7. If you decide to let the knowledge network be reborn, use the existing structure after having assessed it, and use the knowledge and experience gained.

Learning Case

The last activity for Merlin and the network members is to develop external and internal measurements. Consequently, she and the network members must jointly develop a knowledge network scorecard as an external measurement method. They must therefore translate the company's business goal to the network, using a set of indicators. Thereafter the individual goals are again derived from these through the use of a few indicators. The network leader is responsible for the internal measurements, which include the *health check* and the *symptoms of failure*. In order to determine the internal measurement, a *health check* is performed while setting up the network. The network leader is instructed to repeat this periodically. In addition, the network leader also looks for symptoms of failure within and around the network. The individual and role measurements were established beforehand in the development phase of the network (see last section).

	Company	Network	Individual
Financials 	• Sales increase by 10% per year	• Profits resulting from operation of KNN • 10% per year increase in the number of models	• Profits resulting from involvement of Jack Knowly • 10% of input in the innovation process
Customers 	• 25% of products < 3 years	• Increase of 10% in new materials adapted	• 10% increase in new materials used per year
Internal Processes 	• Time to market shortened by 50%	• Time to develop instruments shortened by 50%	• Degree of individual process task fulfillment
Growth 	• Number of patents increased by 10%	• 25% of new ideas generated in comparison to new ideas implemented	• Qualifications, skills, and motivation of employees

Fig. 36. Knowledge scorecard for learning case

Then the scorecard is developed, taking into account that not more than 10-15 indicators should be used in order to stay focused on the desired results. The following indicators (see table above) are chosen in respect of the innovation goal on a company level and especially with reference to the previously mentioned innovation process. They are then translated to the network level and to the individual level, using network member Jack Knowly as an example.

6 Summary and Action Plan

This storyboard part is an activity handbook for practitioners and knowledge managers. It is an applied book that combines knowledge theory with business practices acquired throughout two years of collaboration with our competence center partners: DaimlerChrysler, Hewlett Packard, Lotus, and Unilever. Each section teaches the central concepts and procedures in an important area of the process of building a knowledge network. The handbook may be used in its entirety or in stand-alone parts.

Completing this handbook has been similar to completing a journey. So many miles have been covered and so many interesting places have been seen, it is hard to remember them all. Each building block in our handbook has a central message or key concept that we feel is definitely worth remembering. Therefore, in this last section, we will provide an action plan in three phases, visualized as a project plan. It aims to first show you the way towards the building up of a knowledge network in terms of prioritization of the activities to be undertaken; and second, summarizes the key points of what has been said.

At the beginning you need to think big, start small, and deliver quickly. You have to focus on a single process or knowledge leverage point and build a solution. This is not necessarily a complete solution, but rather an "exhibition" version that will help to "sell" the knowledge network. We cannot emphasize this point sufficiently – do not try to take on everything at once. Starting small is the best way to prove that you can complete a knowledge network that delivers measurable values. A successful initial project can become the basis for further projects as you build momentum towards the "big picture".

Phase I

- Use the visioning process to create a knowledge vision for your actions. It should reflect the mental map of the organization by reflecting the skills and knowledge that the company currently has, the knowledge the organization ought to have, and finally the kind of knowledge that is needed by the organization's members to achieve the future world in which you want to live
- Identify your strategic business goal: efficiency, innovation, or risk management
- Choose a single business process or a task that you can improve, or a knowledge gap and understand how it works. The point is to pick a definable issue and focus on improving it with better content delivery
- Your stakeholders should be asked to support this process
- Understand the knowledge that is needed. Break the process down to each event that requires action by specific people. At each point you need to identify the people who use information, and the type of information that they use
- Select an appropriate way to act or a way to pick the network option by:
  - step 1: deriving the operative goals from the business goals which in turn have been derived from the business strategy,
  - step 2: or, they can be derived from the competitive situation in the industry.

Phase II

- Select the appropriate network:
  - determine your resources (which people are available; what time resources do they have; what skill sets do they possess).
- Compare the knowledge available with the knowledge needed, and the knowledge work process that has to follow.
- Choose the right network reference type.
- Set up the knowledge network:
  - start to actively involve people,
  - ensure that your justification arguments are explicit and create a communication plan that articulates your missions

and values (for the company, for the team, and for the individual),
  - ensure that the top management is committed and then look for sponsors,
  - start to build your core team (put together a small team first, you can make a great start with only a few people),
  - map the specific goals, tasks, and activities of the network and organize the processes,
  - determine roles and responsibilities by bringing the right people together and organizing meetings and events to obtain the members' commitment.
- Think of appropriate facilitating conditions with which to support people and processes:
  - What kind of organizational tools could support the network?
  - Is there a knowledge-sharing culture in the network and an organizational climate of openness?
  - Encourage experimentation, rather than a blind following of the rules,
  - align goals and performance measures across departments, networks, and individuals.
- Organize the appropriate ICT architecture. Consider:
  - getting the right knowledge to the right people,
  - providing universal access to everyone,
  - providing consistent navigation across many applications, documents, and data sources.

Phase III

- Facilitate the relationship of the network with the "outside world":
  - give thought to forming a knowledge board that regularly assesses the knowledge created by the network,
  - provide a broker to support the internal network initiatives,
  - seek integration and coordination with other functions or initiatives.
- Establish internal measurements:
  - think of appropriate incentives and rewards for the individual or the network,

  - establish internal measurements for the network.
- Take care of pitfalls:
  - look at the dos and don'ts,
  - take care of the critical success and critical failure factors.
- Measure the impact of the knowledge network:
  - develop a knowledge network scorecard as an external measurement method: translate the company's business goals to the network by using a set of indicators, and then derive individual goals from that, again using a few indicators,
  - develop internal measurements: perform a health check (during the set up and thereafter periodically) and look for symptoms of failure,
  - give thought to your strategy if the network should fail.
- Market your efforts:
  - show people how your solution can help them,
  - use your model to communicate the benefits of a knowledge network,
  - this is an effective way to build goodwill, to further assess what must be done, and to understand your operating environment better,
  - communicate the network's achievements and ensure that active network members have your attention.

7 List of Figures

Fig. 1. Research design 14
Fig. 2. Structure of the handbook 15
Fig. 3. Business strategy and knowledge networks 18
Fig. 4. Building blocks of the methodology 20
Fig. 5. Derivation of knowledge network reference types 32
Fig. 6. Layers of a knowledge network 33
Fig. 7. Knowledge work processes 34
Fig. 8. Evolution of knowledge work processes 35
Fig. 9. Phases of the process of sharing/transferring knowledge 37
Fig. 10. Facilitating conditions 39
Fig. 11. Requirements for a knowledge network architecture 48
Fig. 12. Classification model for ICT and organizational tools 49
Fig. 13. Knowledge network ICT architecture 54
Fig. 14. Knowledge networks architecture - basic services 55
Fig. 15. Overview - knowledge network architecture scenarios 57
Fig. 16. Example ASP scenario: Lotus Quickplace 59
Fig. 17. Knowledge network reference types – classification criteria 62
Fig. 18. Characteristics experiencing network 63
Fig. 19. Knowledge operational task experiencing network 64
Fig. 20. Characteristics materializing network 67
Fig. 21. Knowledge operational task materializing network 68
Fig. 22. Characteristics systematizing network 71
Fig. 23. Knowledge operational task systematizing network 72
Fig. 24. Characteristics learning network 75
Fig. 25. Knowledge operational task learning network 76
Fig. 26. Integrated measurement system 83
Fig. 27. The balanced scorecard (Kaplan und Norton, 1992) 85
Fig. 28. The balanced scorecard and knowledge management 86
Fig. 29. Examples of measures 89
Fig. 30. Characteristics and dimensions of networks 93
Fig. 31. Probability relevance matrix 96
Fig. 32. Overview of the storyboard 97
Fig. 33. Content of the knowledge created 114

Fig. 34. Building blocks of the knowledge network measurement system 166
Fig. 35. Internal measurement system 168
Fig. 36. Knowledge scorecard for learning case 176

8 List of Tables

Table 1. Communication and coordination tools 50
Table 2. Organizational and management tools 51
Table 3. Integration and database tools 52
Table 4. Intelligent tools 53
Table 5. Pros and cons of the portal-based knowledge network scenario 58
Table 6. Pros and cons of the ASP knowledge network scenario 60
Table 7. Pros and cons of the ubiquitous knowledge network scenario.. 61
Table 8. Organizational tools for experiencing networks 65
Table 9. Organizational and ICT tools for materializing networks 69
Table 10. Organizational and ICT tools for systematizing networks 73
Table 11. Organizational and ICT tools for learning networks 77
Table 12. Dimensions of performance 84
Table 13. Failures and mistakes in networks clustered by characteristics/dimensions of networks 94
Table 14. Failures and mistakes in network that can not be directly influenced 95
Table 15. Matrix with which to select the appropriate network reference type 120
Table 16. Responsibilities, tasks and targets of a specific role 131
Table 17. Potential steps and their adaptation regarding network failures 172
Table 18. Potential action steps regarding failures/mistakes outside the network 173

9 Index

A

ABB 27, 37
Accenture 73
Aerospace 22
Arthur Andersen 35

B

Balanced Scorecard..... 56, 84, 85
Buckman Laboratories 78
Building Blocks 15, 17, 20
Business Strategy.... 8, 17, 18, 21

C

Chevron.................................... 9
Combination 25, 31
Competence Center Knowledge
Networks 14

D

DaimlerChrysler 14

E

Eisai 23, 38
Experiencing Network 19, 32,
..........62ff, 115, 131, 140, 146
Explicit Knowledge 3, 40
Externalization 25, 30, 61

F

Facilitating Conditions 17, 34,
.........................38, 39, 40, 115

H

Health-Check............. 17, 90, 167
HP...................................... 14, 36

I

IBM Global Services 11
ICT Architecture 144
ICT Tools 49, 50, 51, 144
Implicit Knowledge.............. 3, 40
Innovation 22
Internal Measurement.... 156, 168
Internalization 25, 31, 61

K

Knowledge Creation.. 25, 37, 115
Knowledge Flow 24
Knowledge Network ... 7, 18, 122
Advantages 29
Disadvantages 30
Performance 78
Knowledge Network
Architecture 17, 34, 47, 48
Knowledge Network Handbook..
.... 13, 15

Knowledge Network Reference Type..........15, 17, 19, 30ff, 61
Experiencing .... *see .... Experiencing Network*
Learning .... *see Learning .... Network*
Materializing .... *see .... Materializing Network*
Resystematizing .... *see .... Resystematizing Network*
Knowledge Network Scorecard 17, 19, 79, 82, 86
Knowledge Operational Task 19, 26, 30
Knowledge Sharing..... 25, 31, 77
Knowledge Strategy............. 103
Knowledge Transfer .. 23, 25, 27, ... 31, 67
Knowledge Work Processes....................... 17, 34

L

Learning Case .... 111, 120, ... 163, 175
Learning Network...... 19, 32, 74, ... 76, 77, 117, 134, 143, 149
Lotus Professional Services 14
Lotus Quickplace 58

M

Materializing Network..... 19, 32, ...66ff, 116, 132, 142, 146
McKinsey......................... 8, 156
Microsoft.............. 35, 44, 56, 58

O

Organizational Tools...... 49ff, 53

P

Performance Measurement.......... ....56, 81

R

Reference Mode 112, 113, 115
Research Model....................... 14
Resystematizing Network ...... 19, ...32,116, 133, 142, 147
Roles..................................... 128

S

Scenarios 57
Asp-based Knowledge Network........................... 58
Portal-based Knowledge Network..................... 57, 58
Ubiquitous Knowledge Network........................... 60
Seven Eleven Japan................. 66
Sharp 38, 70
Skandia................................... 44
Socialization 25, 30, 61
Stakeholder Analysis............. 106
Success Factors 161, 162
Systematizing Network .... 70 ff

T

Texas Instruments 21

U

Unilever.................................. 14

10 References

Aboody, D. and Baruch, L. (1998). The Value Relevance of Intangibles: Case of Software Capitalization, Working Paper, New York Universtiy Stern School of Business Accounting Departement and University of California at Los Angeles.

Anthes, G. H. (1998). Learning How to Share. Computerworld. 23. February: 75-77.

Arveson, P. (1999). The Balanced Scorecard and Knowledge Management, http://www.balancedscorecard.org/bscand/bsckm.html.

Badaracco, J. L. (1991). The Knowledge Link - How Firms Compete through Strategic Alliances. Boston, Harvard Business School Press.

Barth, M., Clement, M., Foster, G. and Kasznik, R. (1998a). Brand Values and Capital Market Valuation. Working Paper Series, Stanford Graduate School of Business.

Barth, M. and Clinch, G. (1998). Revalued Financial, Tangible and Intangible Assets: Associations with Share Prices and Non-Market - Based Value Estimates. Working Paper Series, Stanford School of Business.

Barth, M., McNichols, M. and Kasznik, R. (1998b). Analyst Coverage and Intangible Assets. Working Paper Series, Stanford Graduate School of Business.

Baruch, L. and Zarowin, P. (1998). The Boundaries of Financial Reporting and How to Extend Them. Working Paper, New York University Stern School of Business Accounting Departement.

Birkett, W. P. (1995). Management Accounting and Knowledge Management. Management Accounting. November: 44-48.

Bleicher, K. (1991). Das Konzept Integriertes Management. Frankfurt.

Botero, I. M. (1995). Company Success is Tied to Human Values. Business Journal Serving Phoenik & the Valley of the Sun. 16.

Brown, J. S. and Duguid, P. (1991). Organizational Learning and Communities-of-Practice: Toward a unified View of Working, Learning and Innovation. Organizational Science. 2 (1): 40-57.

Brown, J. S. and Duguid, P. (1998). Organizing Knowledge. California Management Review. 40 (3): 90-111.

Bryan, L. (1997). Stocks Overvalued? Not in the New Economy. The Wall Street Journal. 40 (3): 90-111.

Bühner, R. and Atitürk, D. (2000). Die Mitarbeiter mit einer Scorecard führen. Harvard Business Manager. 4: 43-53.

Bukowitz, W. and Williams, R. L. (1999). The Knowledge Managment Fieldbook. Harlow, Pearson Education Ltd.

Cohen, W. M. and Levinthal, D. A. (1990). Absorptive Capacity: A New Perspective on Learning and Innovation. Administrative Science Quarterly. 35: 128-152.

Collins, D. J. (1996). Organizational Capability as a Source of Profit. Organizational Learning and Competitive Advantage. Moingeon, E. and Edmondson, A. London, Sage.

Czichos, R. (1990). Change-Management: Konzepte, Prozesse, Werkzeuge für Manager, Verkäufer, Berater und Trainer. München; Basel, E. Reinhardt.

DaimlerChrysler (2000). Interview with a Member of the Community of Practice on Corporate Level about Knowledge Management.

Davenport, T. H. and Prusak, L. (1998). Working Knowledge: How Organizations Manage What They Know. Boston, Harvard Business School Press.

Deng, Z. and Baruch, L. (1997). The Emerging Market for Intangibles. Working Paper, New York University Stern School of Business Accounting Departement.

Deng, Z. and Baruch, L. (1998). The Valuation of Acquired R&D. Working Paper, New York University Stern School of Business Accounting Departement.

Dove, R. (1996). Agile Knowledge Transfer: Reusable, Reconfigurable, Scalable,. Automotive production. 108.

Eberle, F. (2000). Informations- und Kommunikationstechnologien zur Unterstützung von Lernprozessen - Versprechungen, Potentiale, Grenzen. Dienstleistungskompetenz und innovative Geschäftsmodelle. St. Gallen, Thexis: 376-396.

Ellis, R. K. and Hall, L. W. M. (1994). Systems & Values, an Approach for Practical Organizational Intervention. ISSS94 Conference Paper.

Enkel, E. and Wicki, Y. (2002). How Knowledge Networks in Practice Look Like: Findings from an International Survey. KnowledgeSource paper series BE HSG / IWI 3 No. 27. Back, A. and von Krogh, G.

Forbes (1999). Gilder's Publications. Forbes ASAP, http://www.forbes.com/asap /gilder.

Foster, F. (1999). How to Make Communities Work for You. KMWorld. March 1999.

GartnerGroup (1999a). From ISP to ASP: What it Takes to Succeed, and Who Will, GartnerGroup.

GartnerGroup (1999b). Strategic Analysis Report: The Impact of Knowledge Management on Enterprise Architecture, GartnerGroup.

GartnerGroup (1999c). Using an ASP: What are the Risks and Benefits?, GartnerGroup.

Ghalayini, A. M. and Noble, J. S. (1996). The Changing Basis of Performance Measurement. International Journal of Operations & Production Management. 16 (8): 63-80.

Giddens, A. (1984). The Constitution of Society : Outline of the Theory of Structuration. Berkeley, University of California Press.

Gierkink, T. and Ruggles, R. (1997). Leveraging Knowledge for Business Value: Creating Living Knowledge Representations through the Power of Communities, MKO Library, http://www.businessinnovation.ey.com.

Grant, R. M. (1996). Toward a Knowledge-based Theory of the Firm. Strategic Management Journal. 17 (Winter Special Issue): 109-122.

Haerem, T., von Krogh, G. and Roos, J. (1996). Knowledge-Bases Strategic Change. Managing Knowledge. Perspectives on cooperation and competition. von Krogh, G. and Roos, J. London, Thousand Oaks, New Delhi: 116-136.

Hall, L. W. M. (1995). Reducing Complexity: Laying the Groundwork for a New Methodology Based on Hierarchy Theory and Human Values Theory. ISSS95 Conference Paper.

Hamel, G., Doz, Y. L. and Prahalad, C. K. (1989). Collaborate with Your Competitors - and Win. Harvard Business Review. January-February: 133-139.

Hammer, M. and Champy, J. (1993). Reengineering the Corporation. New York, Harper Business.

Hanley, S. S. (1999). Knowledge-based Communities of Practice at AMS.

Hansen, M. T., Nohira, N. and Tierney, T. (1999). What's Your Strategy for Managing Knowledge ? Harvard Business Review. 77 (2): 106-116.

Hart, L. (1995). In knowledge economy emphasis is on thinking. Atlanta Business Chronicle. 18.

Haythornthwaite, C. (1999). Online Personal Networks: Size, Composition and Media Use among Distance Learners, http://alexia.lis.uiuc.edu/~haythorn/Ego.html. 10.08.2000.

Högberg, C. and Edvinson, L. (1998). A Design for Futurizing Knowledge Networking. Journal of Knowledge Management. 2 (2): 81-92.

Huber, N. (1998). Environmental Warning: Swinson Calls for Review of Annual Reports with Focus on Intangible Assets. Accountancy Age. Sept. 17th.

IDC (1999). Knowledge Management Survey, http://collateral.pok.ibm.com/fasttrack/pdffiles/Lotus(6pg).pdf.

Inkpen, A. C. (1996). Creating Knowledge through Collaboration. California Management Review. 39 (1): 123-140.

Inkpen, A. C. and Crossan, M. M. (1995). Believing is Seeing: Joint Ventures and Organization Learning. Journal of Management Studies. 32 (5): 595-618.

Kaplan, R. S. and Norton, D. P. (1992). The Balanced Scorecard - Measures that Drive Perfomance. Harvard Business Review. 70 (1): 71-79.

Kaplan, R. S. and Norton, D. P. (1996). The Balanced Scorecard: Translating Strategy into Action. Boston, Harvard Business School Press.

Kim, A. J. (2000). Community Building on the Web. Berkeley, CA, Peachpit Press.

Klepper, R. and Hoffman, N. (2000). Assimilation of New Information Technology and Organizational Culture: A Case Study. Wirtschaftsinformatik. 42 (4): 339-346.

Kogut, B. and Zander, U. (1993). Knowledge of the Firm and the Evolutionary Theory of the Multinational Corporation. Journal of International business Studies. 23 (4): 625-645.

Köhne, M., Enkel, E., Seufert, A., Back, A. and von Krogh, G. (2000). Development Aspects and Supportive Factors in Knowledge Networks, BE HSG/ IWI Nr. 18.

KPMG Germany (1999). Wissensmanagement, http://www.kpmg.de.

Kriwet, C. K. (1997). Inter- and Intraorganizational Knowledge Transfer. Bamberg.

Lam, A. (1997). Embedded Firms, Embedded Knowledge: Problems of Collaboration and Knowledge Transfer in Global Cooperative Ventures. Organization Sudies. 18 (6): 973-996.

Leadbeater, C. (1998). Time to Let the Bean-Counters Go. The Statesman. (April 17).

Lehner, F. (2000). Organisational Memory. Konzepte und Systeme für das organisatorische Lernen und das Wissensmanagement. München, Hanser.

Leonard, D. and Sensiper, S. (1998). The Role of Tacit Knowledge in Group Innovation. California Management Review. 40 (3): 112-132.

Leonard-Barton, D. (1995). Wellsprings of Knowledge: Building and Sustaining the Sources of Innovation. Boston, Harvard Business School Press.

Letza, S. R. (1996). The Design and Implementation of the Balanced Scorecard. An Analysis of Three Companies in Practice. Business Process Reengineering & Management Journal. 2 (3): 54-76.

Lloyd, B. (1998). Understanding the Power, Responsibility, Leadership and Learning Links: The Key to Successful Knowledge Management. Journal of Systemic Knowledge Management.

Lotus (1999). Raven Overview.

Lotus Development Corporation (2000). Lotus Quickplace 2.0: Overview Brochure, http://www.lotus.com/home.nsf/welcome/quickplace. 24.08.2000.

McDermott, R. (1995). Designing and Improving Knowledge Work. Journal for Quality and Participation. 18 (2): 72-77.

Mentzas, G. and Apostolou, D. (1998). Towards a Holistic Knowledge Leveraging Infrastructure: The KNOWNET Approach. Second International Vonference on Practical Aspects of Knowledge Management, Basel, Switzerland.

Merkle, M. (1999). Bewertung von Unternehmensnetzwerken: Eine empirische Bestandsaufnahme mit der Balanced Scorecard. St. Gallen, University of St. Gallen.

Miles, R. C. and Snow, C. C. (1986). Network Organizations: New Concepts for New Forms. California Management Review. 34 (53-72).

Nonaka, I. (1991). The Knowledge-Creating Company. Harvard Business Review. 69 (6): 96-104.

Nonaka, I. (1992). Wie japanische Konzerne Wissen erzeugen. HARVARDmanager. 2: 95-103.

Nonaka, I. (1999). Leading Knowledge Creation (plenary Speech). 32nd Hawaii International Conference on System Sciences, Maui, Hawaii.

Nonaka, I. and Konno, N. (1998). The Concept of "Ba": Building a Foundation for Knowledge Creation. California Management Review. 40. (3): 40-55.

Nonaka, I., Reinmoeller, P. and Senoo, D. (1998). The Art of Knowledge: Systems to Capitalize on Market Knowledge. European Management Journal. 16 (6): 673-684.

Nonaka, I. and Takeuchi, H. (1995). The Knowledge Creating Company: How Japanese Companies Create the Dyamics of Innovation. New York/ Oxford, Oxford University Press.

O'Dell, C. and Grayson, C. (1998). If only We Knew What We Know - Identification and Transfer of Internal Best Practices. California Management Review. 40 (3): 154-174.

Porter, M. E. (1985). Competitive Advantage. New York, The Free Press.

Powell, W. (1998). Learning from Collaboration: Knowledge and Networks in the Biotechnology and Pharmaceutical Industries. California Management Review. 40 (3): 228-241.

Prahalad, C. K. and Hamel, G. (1990). The Core Competence of the Corporation. Harvard Business Review. 68 (3): 79-91.

Probst, G., Raub, S. and Romhardt, K. (1999). Wissen managen. Wie Unternehmen ihre erfolgreichste Ressource optimal nutzen. Frankfurt/Main, Frankfurter Allgemeine Zeitung.

Process Edge Technologies (1998). A White Paper on Knowledge Management and Corporate Culture, http://www.processedge.com.

Raimann, J., Enkel, E., Seufert, A., Back, A. and von Krogh, G. (2000). Supporting Business Processes through Knowledge Management. Working Paper Research Center KnowledgeSource, University of St. Gallen. BE HSG/ IWI 3 Nr. 14/ IfB Nr. 42.

Ruggles, R. L. (1997). Tools for Knowledge Management: an Introduction. Knowledge Management Tools. Ruggles, R. L. Newton, Butterworth-Heinemann.

Schmid, B. and Lindemann, M. (1998). Elements of a Reference Model for Electronic Markets. 31st HICSS, Hawaii.

Schüppel, J. (1996). Wissensmanagement: Organisatorisches Lernen im Spannungsfeld von Wissens- und Lernbarrieren. Dissertation. Wiesbaden., Gabler.

Senge, P. (1994). The Fifth Discipline: The Art and Practice of Learning Organization. New York, New York, Currency Doubleday.

Seufert, A., Back, A. and von Krogh, G. (1999). A Vision for Knowledge Networking. Working Paper Research Center KnowledgeSource, University of St. Gallen. BE HSG/ IWI 3 Nr. 10/ IfB Nr. 39.

Seufert, A. and Seufert, S. (1999). The Genius Approach: Building Learning Networks for Advanced Management Education. 32nd Hawaii International Conference on System Sciences, 05.-08.01.1999, Maui, Hawaii.

Seufert, S., Back, A. and Häusler, M. (2001). E-Learning: Weiterbildung im Internet, Das "Plato-Cookbook" für internetbasiertes Lernen. Kilchberg, SmartBooks Publishing AG.

Skyrme, D. J. (1999). Knowledge Networking. Creating the Collaborative Enterprise. Oxford.

Staehle, W. H. (1999). Management. München, Vahlen.

Stewart, T. A. (1991). Brainpower: How Intellectual Capital is Becoming Amer.

Stewart, T. A. (1994). Your Company's most Valuable Asset: Intellectual Capital. FORTUNE. (October 3): 68-74.

Stewart, T. A. (1995a). Mapping Corporate Brainpower. FORTUNE. (October 30): 209-211.

Stewart, T. A. (1995b). Trying to Grasp the Intagible. FORTUNE. (October 2): 157-161.

Szulanski, G. (1994). Unpacking Stickiness: An Empircial Investigation of the Barriers to Transfer Best Practices inside the Firm.

Tanuan, M. C. (1997). An Introduction to Workflow and Business Process Modeling, http://www.grad.-math.uwaterloo.ca/~mctanuan/cs645/IntroBPMWF.htm.

The Know-Net Consortium (2000). Know-Net.ORG, http://www.know-net.org. 24.08.2000.

Vassiliadis, S. (1999). Internal Presentation: Measurements of Intellectual Capital and Knowledge.

Vassiliadis, S., Seufert, A., Back, A. and von Krogh, G. (2000). Competing with Intellectual Capital. Working Paper Research Center KnowledgeSource, University of St. Gallen. BE HSG/ IWI 3 Nr. 15/ IfB Nr. 43.

Vassiliadis, S., Wicki, Y., Seufert, A., Back, A. and von Krogh, G. (1999). Knowledge Networks. Linking Knowledge Management to Business Strategy. Working Paper Research Center KnowledgeSource, University of St. Gallen. BE HSG/ IWI 3 Nr. 11/ IfB Nr. 40.

von Krogh, G. (1999). Internal Presentation. University of St. Gallen.

von Krogh, G., Ichijo, K. and Nonaka, I. (1998). Bringing Care into Knowledge Creation of Business Organizations. Knowledge Creation. Nonaka, I. and Nishigushi, T., Oxford Universtiy Press.

von Krogh, G., Ichijo, K. and Nonaka, I. (2000). Enabling Knowledge Creation: How to Unlock the Mystery of Tacit Knowledge and Release the Power of Innovation. New York, New York, Oxford University Press.

von Krogh, G. and Köhne, M. (1998). Der Wissenstransfer in Unternehmen. Phasen des Wissenstransfers und wichtige Einflussfaktoren. Die Unternehmung. Heft 5/6, : 235-252.

von Krogh, G., Nonaka, I. and Aben, M. (1999). Steps to a Knowledge Strategy. IfB. St. Gallen, University St. Gallen.

von Krogh, G., Nonaka, I. and Aben, M. (2001). Making the Most of Your Company's Knowledge: A Strategic Framework. Long Range Planning. 34 (4): 421-439.

von Krogh, G. and Roos, J. (1996). Managing Knowledge. Perspectives on cooperation and competition. London/ Thousand Oaks/New Delhi.

von Krogh, G. and Venzin, M. (1995). Anhaltende Wettbewerbsvorteile durch Wissensmanagement. Die Unternehmung. 95 (6): 417-435.

Wathne, K., Roos, J. and von Krogh, G. (1996). Towards a Theory of Knowledge Transfer in a Cooperative Context. Managing Knowledge. Perspectives on Cooperation and Competition. von Krogh, G. and Roos, J. London, Sage Publications.

Webster, F. E. (1992). The Changing Role of Marketing in the Corporation. Journal of Marketing. 56 (2): 1-17.

Wenger, E. (1998a). Communities of Practice. Learning as a Social System.

Wenger, E. (1998b). Communities of Practice: Learning, Meaning and Identity. Cambridge, Cambridge University Press.

Widmer, G. (1999). Die Rolle von Wissensmanagement bei Diversifikationsstrategien, Diplomarbeit. Universität St. Gallen.

Wireless Knowledge (2000). Workstyle Server: Product Overview White Paper, http://www.wirelessknowledge.com/pdfs/workstyle_wpaper.pdf. 25.08.2000.

Zucker, B. and Schmitz, C. (1994). Wissen nutzen statt verspielen. Gablers Magazin. 11-12: 62-65.

Printing and Binding: Strauss GmbH, Mörlenbach